MW01075678

The

ORTHODOXY

of the

CHURCH

WATCHMAN NEE

Living Stream Ministry
Anaheim, California

Second Edition, May 1994.

ISBN 0-87083-007-4

Published by
Living Stream Ministry
1853 W. Ball Road, Anaheim, CA 92804 U.S.A.
P. O. Box 2121, Anaheim, CA 92814 U.S.A.

Printed in the United States of America

97 98 99 00 01 02 / 9 8 7 6 5 4 3 2

CONTENTS

THE ORTHODOXY OF
THE CHURCH

PREFACE TO THE ENGLISH EDITION

I have never met a servant of the Lord so balanced as Brother Watchman Nee. He is rich in life, and he is also rich in knowledge. He knows and loves the Lord, and he knows and loves the Bible too. He knows Christ, and he also knows the church. He is for Christ, and he is also for the church. Thus, his ministry has been always balanced with two sides—the spiritual and the practical. Books such as *The Normal Christian Life; Sit, Walk, Stand; What Shall This Man Do?; The Spiritual Man; The Release of the Spirit; The Song of Songs; Love Not the World; The God of Abraham, Isaac, and Jacob; The Glorious Church;* and many others which have not yet been translated into English contain messages given by him on the spiritual side. On the practical side, there are *The Assembly Life* (messages given and published in 1934), *The Normal Christian Church Life* (messages given in 1937 and published in 1938), *The Orthodoxy of the Church* (messages given and published in 1945), *Further Talks on the Church Life* (messages given and published within the period of 1948 through 1951), and *Church Affairs* (messages given in 1948 and published in 1949-1950). The messages on the spiritual side are principally concerned with the matters of spiritual life, while those on the practical side are absolutely concerned with the practice of the church life, i.e., the way to practice the church life. Spiritual life, of course, is vital to us. But the practice of the church life is also necessary. Most Christians pay much attention to the spiritual life but neglect the practice of the church. Some Christian teachers even stress the spiritual life but oppose the practice of the church life. Brother Nee, however, is adequately balanced in these two matters. He not only takes the commission of the spiritual life, but also bears the burden of the practice of the church life. He has a clear vision of both, and he is faithful to the Lord for the spiritual life as well as honest to His people regarding the practice of the church life. He realizes that even if we are rich in the spiritual life but do not have the proper practice of the church life, we are still short of the purpose of God. Therefore, he emphasizes both of these matters. May we also be so balanced and give adequate attention to both sides.

The messages in the book were given and published in 1945 at Chungking. They are exceedingly unveiling and illuminating. Besides many other points, they cover the two main matters: returning to the orthodoxy of the church and taking the ground of locality, which is the unique ground of genuine unity.

Some think that the ground of locality is something of the Brethren teaching and that we have adopted this kind of teaching from the Brethren. In fact, the Brethren have never seen the ground of locality and have never used the term *the ground of unity*. In chapter seven of this book, Brother Nee says:

> The brothers did not see the "local" ground and boundary of the church.... [They] have not noticed the oneness of each and every local church in each and every locality as recorded in the Bible.

And again:

> The Brethren did not pay enough attention to the fact that the church has the locality as her boundary....The "Exclusive Brethren" exceed the boundary of locality, while the "Open Brethren" are smaller than the boundary of locality. They forget that in the Bible there is one and only one church in every locality.

Still further he says:

> The difficulty of the Brethren...was that they were not clear enough regarding the teaching in the Bible on locality....Because they have not realized the importance of the teachings in the Bible concerning the locality, divisions have resulted.

There is more which Brother Nee says in this regard which I do not quote here. The ground of locality was not discovered by us until 1937, and that through Brother Nee. Even by 1934, Brother Nee had only discovered the boundary of a local church, which is the boundary of the locality within which a local church is situated. Due to the confusion among the Brethren assemblies (that is, in one city there are several Brethren assemblies) which he saw in 1933, he studied the New Testament once again in order to ascertain the boundary of a local church (assembly). Eventually, he discovered that the New Testament reveals clearly that the boundary of a local church is the boundary of the locality (city) in which the local church stands. Immediately after his new discovery, Brother Nee gave a series of messages on this matter in January of 1934 in Shanghai, and these were published in the same year as the book *The Assembly Life.* Thus, in his messages and publications subsequent to that time, he began to use the term *the boundary of locality,* not yet the term *the ground of locality.*

Then, based upon the boundary of locality, Brother Nee came to see the ground of locality. Since the boundary of a local church is the boundary of the locality in which it stands, so the ground of the church must be the ground of the locality on which a local church is built. This is the unique ground which keeps the genuine unity of the church. Any ground other than this is divisive. After he saw this, Brother Nee called a workers' conference in January of 1937 in Shanghai to pass on this clear vision of the proper church ground to his fellow workers. The same series of messages was given again to the co-workers in the fall of the same year at Hankow and was published in 1938 as the book *The Normal Christian Church Life.* Thus, it was in 1937 that the ground of locality was revealed to us and the term *the ground of locality* began to be used among us.

I relate some of the history just to make it clear that the ground of locality is a new discovery, another item of the Lord's recovery in the last days through Brother Nee, not something of the recovery through the Brethren.

We do not care merely for doctrine. We care for the Lord's recovery and the Lord's way. May the Lord's grace bring us up to date in His recovery. May we see the proper ground of the church, which is the ground of locality, the unique ground of genuine unity, that we may have the proper way for the practice of the church life. May we see the vision unveiled in the last seven epistles of the Lord to His church and hear what the Spirit speaks to the churches, that we may not join the Catholic Thyatira, nor stay in the Protestant Sardis, neither fall into the Brethren Laodicea, but absolutely remain in the brotherly-love Philadelphia, which is the church that has returned to the orthodoxy of the apostolic church. What we urgently need today is to come back to the orthodoxy of the beginning and stand firmly on the ground of locality. The time is short! The Lord is coming! May we prepare ourselves to meet Him in and through the proper church life! Amen!

Witness Lee
Los Angeles, California, U.S.A.
November 5, 1969

CHAPTER ONE

INTRODUCTION

Scripture Reading: Rev. 1—3; 22:7, 18-19

The apostle John's writings, whether his Epistles or his Gospel, were always the last in each category. Revelation, of course, was the last of all the books written in the Bible. The Gospels of Matthew, Mark, and Luke were written regarding the behavior of the Lord Jesus on this earth, while the Gospel of John speaks of "He who descended out of heaven, the Son of Man, who is in heaven" (3:13). John wrote at the time when the Gnostics were confusing the Word of God; his writings bring men to heaven to see God's eternal fact in heaven. John brings us out of the realm of man to wholly receive the Son of God. What John wrote has the special feature of bringing us back to the beginning. The Gospel of John tells us that Christ was in the beginning; the Epistles of John speak of the Word of life which was from the beginning; and Revelation brings us to eternity in the future. The Gospel of John shows us the Son of God who was in the flesh—He was in the midst of us, but men mistook Him, thinking that He was only Jesus of Nazareth. Therefore, John showed us that this Jesus who was in the flesh was in the beginning. This is the fact behind the scene. The Epistles of John do likewise. His person is the Son of God, and His office is Christ. But men did not know the Son of God; neither did they know the Christ. So the Epistles of John specially speak of these two points, bringing us back to the fact behind the scene in the beginning. At the time John wrote Revelation, the world was in great confusion, and Caesar of Rome was at his worst. So John brought us into the condition behind the scenes of the future to let us know how God regards the situation of this world. However, in Revelation we see not only the condition of the world, but also the condition of the church. Revelation also shows us what pleases the Lord, what the Lord condemns, and what the Lord's way is for the church, when the outward appearance of the church is extremely confusing. The church in her appearance has many manifestations in history, but what way, what condition, is the Lord's desire? This desire behind the scenes is shown by John.

In the Bible there are two groups of seven epistles. God used Paul to write the first group—Romans, 1 and 2 Corinthians, Galatians, Ephesians, Philippians, Colossians, and 1 and 2 Thessalonians—and God used John to write the second group. The first seven Epistles speak of the church in a time of normality; the latter speak of the churches in a time of abnormality. The three Gospels of Matthew, Mark, and Luke are normal, helping men to know God, but the Gospel of John is God's reaction to man's unclearness; that is why it frequently speaks of truth and grace. John's Epistles were also God's reaction to abnormality; that is why they speak of light and love more often. Revelation 2 and 3 are God's dealings with the abnormal conditions of the churches. The first seven Epistles of Paul deal with the normal behavior of the church. Later, the church was not normal; therefore, John wrote the last seven epistles in Revelation. The first seven Epistles contain the truth the church must know; the last seven epistles show the way the church must take. Today if a man really wants to walk in the Lord's way, he must read Revelation 2 and 3. Today the church has problems; therefore, Revelation tells us what to do. If you do not seek the way in Revelation, I do not know how you can be a Christian.

Furthermore, the first seven Epistles were written before the last hour, while the last seven epistles were written either during or after the last hour. First John 2:18 indicates another time, the last hour. "Young children, it is the last hour; and even as you heard that antichrist is coming, even now many antichrists have come; whereby we know that it is the last hour." If Christians only see the light in the first Epistles, they do not know the will of God in the last hour.

In the Bible there were three persons with outstanding ministries: Peter, John, and Paul. Second Peter was the last book written by Peter. In this Epistle, Peter brought up the matter of apostasy. Second Timothy was the last book written by Paul. Verse 2 of chapter two says, "And the things which you have heard from me through many witnesses, these commit to faithful men, who will be competent to teach others also." First Timothy 3:15 tells us that the church is the house of God, the pillar and base of the truth, but in 2 Timothy 2:20, Paul says, "But in a great house there are not only gold and silver vessels but also wooden and earthen." The problem is whether a man will cleanse himself from the vessels of dishonor to pursue righteousness, faith, love, and peace with those who call on the Lord out of a pure heart (vv. 21-22). The Epistles of John were written by John as his last books. He said that the antichrists had already come and that we must keep the Word of God (1 John 2:18, 24; 4:3). I feel burdened to make this matter clear. Generally speaking, the time from the beginning of the church until now is one age—the age of the church. But the problem is not that simple. The normal and the abnormal must be separated. Today the outward appearance of the church is desolate—if we have not seen this fact, there is no need for us to read Revelation. The first seven Epistles (i.e., those written by Paul) deal with the normal. But now the situation is abnormal. What then should we do?

Indeed, the confusion on the earth does not affect the spiritual reality. God's spiritual reality still remains. But the church in her outward appearance, at least, is confused. The Roman Catholic Church claims that it is the Body of Christ. According to a survey taken in 1914 of Protestantism, there were more than 1500 well-organized denominations, excluding scattered groups, each claiming to be the Body of Christ. Before John, Paul, and Peter passed away, this had already started. Paul wrote to Timothy, saying, "All who are in Asia turned away from me" (2 Tim. 1:15). Even Ephesus was included. In this kind of circumstance, the children of God must seek one thing; that is, how should we follow and serve the Lord? What should we do? When the appearance of the church is desolate, we must ask, "What should we do?" Revelation 2 and 3 give us a way in which to walk. If we are really seeking before God, Revelation 2 and 3 will tell us what to do.

The first thing we must know when coming to read Revelation is what kind of book it is. Everyone knows that it is a book of prophecies, but if we ask whether the seven churches are prophetic, they dare not say. Chapters one through twenty-two show us that the special feature of Revelation is that it is a book of prophecy in nature. Not only are the seven seals, the seven trumpets, and the seven vials prophetic, but even the seven epistles are prophetic. This book is a book of prophecy. That is why no one dares add anything to it, nor is anyone allowed to take anything from it. Since it is a book of prophecy, we must treat it as prophecy and discover the fulfillment of its prophecy. The nature of the book of Revelation, we must note, is firstly prophetic; secondly, since it is prophecy, it will be fulfilled. At that time there were more than seven churches in Asia. Why then did John speak of only these seven? When he was on the isle of Patmos, he saw only these seven churches because these seven represent all the others. God chose seven churches which have characteristics of mutual affinity and put the prophecy on them.

On the earth there are seven churches; in heaven there are only seven lampstands. Here is a problem: Whenever there is a church on the earth, there is a lampstand in heaven. The strange thing is that John saw only seven lampstands in heaven. Are there then only seven churches on the earth? It seems that the church in Chungking has been cut off, and the church in Nanking has also been cut off. What should we do? This is why we must remember that this is prophecy. Since it is prophecy, only seven churches were selected. These seven churches are representative of all other churches; there is no number eight to be represented. There are more than seven churches on earth, but these seven are selected as representatives. There are only seven lampstands in heaven, because the history of the seven churches constitutes the complete history of the church.

We must give special heed to the word in chapter one: "Blessed is he who reads and those who hear the words of the prophecy and keep the things written in it" (v. 3). Revelation 22:7 also says, "Blessed is he who keeps the words of the prophecy of this scroll." We may say that this prophecy is God's commandments. Although outwardly this book is clothed with prophecy, inwardly it is the commandment of God. This is a book for practice, not for study. The prophecy here differs from other prophecies; this one is for man to keep. Between John and us there is a common principle; that is, this prophecy is for us to keep—to keep from beginning to end. How can those who do not want to keep it understand Revelation? How can they understand the seven churches?

In reading Revelation 2 and 3, we must see not only that this is a prophecy for us to keep, but also that the Lord is the Lord of judgment. The first half of Revelation 1 is the preface to the whole book of Revelation; the last half is the preface to chapters two and three. These two chapters start with the revelation of the Lord Jesus. In 1:13 we see the Lord "clothed with a garment reaching to the feet." The priests wore long garments; here the Lord is the High Priest. The lampstand is in the Holy Place, the light of which will not be extinguished. Its light burns day and night; therefore, the priest must continually trim it and add oil to it in the Holy Place. The Lord Jesus is the High Priest who walks in the midst of the churches to see which lamp is lighted and which one is not. The trimming is the judgment, because judgment begins in the house of God. Christ walks in the midst of the churches doing the work of judgment, and today's judgment is seen from eternity.

John was the one who was closest to the Lord, because he leaned on the Lord's breast (John 21:20, 24). The Son is in the bosom of the Father, and John was in the bosom of the Son. Yet the day he saw the Lord, he fell at His feet as dead, because He is the Judge. Formerly, we saw Him as the Lord of grace; now we see Him as the Lord of judgment. But the judgment here is the judgment of a priest, for it involves *trimming*. On that day it will be entirely judgment. Every one of God's children must one day meet the Lord's fearfulness and holiness; then they will no longer reason. Light disposes of all reasons—it not only illuminates; it also kills. The illumination in every part of the Bible kills the natural life of man. Men may have many reasons, but before the Lord they are all gone. All men will fall dead to the ground just as John did. The farther a person is from the Lord, the greater is his self-confidence; but it is impossible for him to bear the light of God. We must be dealt with by God at least once.

The first part of each epistle tells us who the Lord is, and the word that follows is based on this revelation of the Lord. He who does not know the Lord cannot see the church. The church is the continuation of the cross; there is no such thing as knowing the cross yet not knowing the extension of the cross.

These seven epistles start with the Lord and end with the call to the overcomers. Who are the overcomers? What are the overcomers? Are they special ones, those who are above the ordinary? In the Bible the meaning of the overcomers is that they are the normal, ordinary ones. Those who are not abnormal during the time of abnormality are the overcomers. Most people are below this level. The overcomers are not above this level, but at this level. God is calling the overcomers today to rise up and walk according to the normal pattern in the beginning. The will of God never changes; it is just like a straight line. Today men fall, fail, and continually go downward; but the overcomers are recovered anew into the will of God.

Here we see two more matters: First, the church is the golden lampstand, and the Lord walks in the midst of the lampstands; second, the Lord holds the seven stars in His right hand, which are the angels of the seven churches.

Each of the various kinds of metals spoken of in the Bible has meaning: iron typifies political power, brass typifies judgment, silver typifies redemption, and gold typifies the glory of God. The glory of God is one thing that no one knows or comprehends. Although it is difficult to comprehend the holiness of God, we can still comprehend it. The righteousness of God can also be understood. But the glory of God has never been known, because it is the one characteristic that belongs most uniquely to God. The church is made of gold. The people in the church are born of God, not of blood, not of the will of the flesh, nor of the will of man. The church has absolutely nothing to do with man. Some ask what the work of wood, grass, and stubble is. Wood, grass, and stubble are the works of the flesh. The work of gold, silver, and precious stones is that which is entirely of God.

These seven epistles were written to the angels of the seven churches, differing from the first seven Epistles written by Paul. Paul wrote to the churches, although we see that there were all the saints, overseers, and deacons, especially in the book to the Philippians. Here the epistles were written to the angels of the seven churches, not directly to the churches. However, they were the words spoken by the Holy Spirit to the churches. The seven stars are the angels of the seven churches. The word *angel* in Greek is *angelos*. This word represents one who is a messenger. Many people, after reading Revelation 2 and 3, have tried to find similarities between the last seven epistles and the first seven and have injected all manner of wrong explanations regarding the messengers. Who is this messenger? The messenger spoken of here is singular in number; the epistles were written to a singular messenger. However, this singular number is corporate in nature; that is why, at the end of each epistle, the calling is to the overcomers in plural. This messenger is a corporate messenger who can represent a minority in the whole church. At this point the way of God is different. Formerly, the church stood before the Lord; now the messenger stands before the Lord. The light of the lamp is inferior to the light of the star. The Lord has chosen the inextinguishable starlight and said that this is His messenger. This star is in the Lord's hand. Today a group of people is a messenger in the eyes of the Lord; thus, the nature of the church today is entrusted to them. When the church has a problem before the Lord in her outward appearance, the Lord sees a group of people—a messenger—who can be the representative of the church. Formerly, the representatives of the church were the elders with position and office; now the responsibility of representing the church is given to the spiritual messenger. This messenger is not necessarily the elders or deacons. Today God places the responsibility upon whoever can represent the church. Those who can represent the church have the responsibility committed to them by God. Today it is not a matter of position and office, but of having real spiritual authority before God—to such ones God turns over the responsibility.

Revelation is written to the "slaves" of God. Therefore, unless you are a slave, you will not be able to understand. He who is not bought with the blood and constrained by love to be a slave cannot understand Revelation.

John wrote Revelation in A.D. 95 or 96 at the time Domitian was Caesar in Rome. Of the twelve apostles, John was the last to die; therefore, the church of the apostles ended with John. When John was writing, the seven epistles were prophetic. Today when we read the seven epistles, we also must regard them as prophecy. However, when we consider them today, they have already become history. John was looking ahead, while we are looking back.

Now we will look at the seven churches in the seven epistles one by one.

CHAPTER TWO

THE CHURCH IN EPHESUS

Scripture Reading: Rev. 2:1-7

The church in Ephesus is prophetic concerning the condition of the first stage of the church after the apostles. The apostolic age was prior to A.D. 96. After A.D. 96 the apostolic age apparently was over, and many wrong things began to creep in. Since Revelation is a book of prophecy, the names in the book are also prophetic. *Ephesus* in Greek means "desirable." The church which continued after the apostolic church was still desirable.

"I know your works and your labor and your endurance" (Rev. 2:2a). The pronoun *your* in Revelation 2 and 3 is singular in number. Among the seven churches, five are rebuked, one receives no rebuke and no praise, and only one is praised. Ephesus is one among those which are rebuked. But the Lord first tells the messenger of Ephesus about the spiritual reality. Some think the Lord attempts to say something good before He rebukes so that the one being rebuked will not feel so bad, as if the Lord is being diplomatic. But this is not so with the Lord. Rather, the Lord points out the spiritual reality in the church. There is something called the spiritual reality which exists regardless of the outward condition. Although the Israelites were worthless in the sight of men, God said through Balaam that He did not behold iniquity in Jacob (Num. 23:21). It is not that God does not look; rather, He looks but sees nothing wrong. It is not that the eyes of God can see better than ours, but that God sees the spiritual reality.

It is not difficult for us to see that the condition of the church today is desolate. Sometimes we think a certain brother or sister is just as desolate. But if the children of

God are enlightened by the Lord, they will see that their many weaknesses and failures are lies. If the spiritual reality is true, then these are all lies. Consider a little child who runs out to the street and returns covered with mud. Although he is filthy when he enters the house, I say that he is clean and beautiful. It is true that his body is covered with dirt, but the dirt does not grow out of him. Once he is washed, he will be clean again. Each child of God must see that even before he is washed, he is good. The dirtiness is a lie; his reality is good. Today the church does not *look* as glorious as God says, but today the church *is* glorious. If you have spiritual insight, though the church is not washed, you can still see that she is good. For this reason you can also thank God continually for the church. Today the church is glorious, not having spot or wrinkle or any such things (Eph. 5:25-27). No spot means sinless, and no wrinkle means not aged, always maintaining her freshness before the Lord. God says the church in Ephesus is good; it is her spiritual reality that is good.

"And you have tried those who call themselves apostles and are not, and have found them to be false" (Rev. 2:2b). The Lord says something about trying the apostles, which proves that after the apostolic age there are still apostles in the church. If there were only twelve apostles, then all they would have to ask is whether or not the professed apostle was John. If he was not John, then he would not be an apostle, because by that time all the other eleven apostles had passed away and only John was left. The necessity for the apostles to be tried proves that there were still more apostles after the twelve apostles.

"But I have one thing against you, that you have left your first love" (v. 4). The word "first" in Greek is *proten*. It refers not only to primacy in time but also in nature. In Luke 15 the father gave the *best* robe to the prodigal son to put on; the word "best" is also *proten*.

"But if not, I am coming to you and will remove your lampstand out of its place, unless you repent" (Rev. 2:5b). The churches in Revelation 2 and 3 are not only churches in prophecy but also churches that were actually in seven localities in Asia. Remarkably, history tells us that for more than a thousand years, there has been no church in Ephesus. The lampstand has been removed; even her outward appearance has been removed. Now there are churches in Corinth, Rome, and so forth, but none in Ephesus. Because she did not repent, the lampstand was removed.

"*But this you have, that you hate the works of the Nicolaitans, which I also hate*" (v. 6). Nicolaitans cannot be found in church history. Since Revelation is a book of prophecy, we must look into the meaning of the word. *Nicolait* in Greek is composed of two words. *Nikao* means "conquer" or "above others." *Laos* means "common people," "secular people," or "laity." So *nicolait* means "conquering the common people," "climbing above the laity." Nicolaitans, then, refers to a group of people who esteem themselves higher than the common believers. The Lord is above; the common believers are below. The Nicolaitans are below the Lord yet above the common believers. The Lord hates the behavior of the Nicolaitans. The conduct of climbing over and above the common believers as a mediatorial class is what the Lord detests; it is something to be hated. But at that time there was only the behavior; it had not yet become a teaching.

In the New Testament there is a fundamental principle: All of the children of God are priests of God. In Exodus 19:5-6 God called unto the people of Israel, saying, "Now therefore, if ye will obey my voice indeed, and keep my covenant, then ye shall be a peculiar treasure unto me above all people: for all the earth is mine: and ye shall be unto me a kingdom of priests, and a holy nation." God ordained in the beginning that the whole nation be priests, but the incident of worshipping the golden calf occurred not long after. Moses broke the tables of law and said, "Who is on the Lord's side? let him come unto me....And slay every man his brother" (32:26-27). At that time the Levites came to stand on the Lord's side, and as a result, three thousand Israelites were slain on that day (v. 28). Henceforth, only the Levites could be priests; the kingdom of priests became a tribe of priests. The rest of the people of Israel could not be priests, and they had to depend on the Levites to be the priests on their behalf.

The priestly class in the Old Testament was a mediatorial class. However, in the New Testament, Peter said, "But you are a chosen race, a royal priesthood, a holy nation, a people acquired for a possession" (1 Pet. 2:9). We, the whole church, are priests; this goes back to the condition in the beginning. Revelation 1:5-6 says that as many as are washed in the blood are priests. The priests are in charge of God's business; every believer is in charge of God's business. There should not be a mediatorial class in the church. The church has only one High Priest, the Lord Jesus.

Before a change took place in the church, all the believers took care of the Lord's business. But after the apostles, this condition began to change; men began to lose interest in the matter of serving the Lord. When the Roman Catholic Church began (in the time of Pergamos), there were few who were saved but many who were baptized; thus, unbelievers filled the church. Then there appeared a group of "clergy." Since there were members who were not spiritual, what could they do? Asking them to put down the account books and pick up the Bible to preach would not be fitting. So a group of people was sought out to take special care of spiritual affairs while the rest did secular work. Thus, the "clergy" was produced contrary to God's desire. God desires that all who do secular work should also take care of spiritual affairs.

In the Roman Catholic Church, the dispensing of the bread, the laying on of hands, baptizing, etc., are all performed by the Catholic priests; even weddings and funerals must be undertaken by the "clergy." In the Protestant church there are pastors. For illness, call the doctor; for lawsuits, call the lawyer; for spiritual affairs, call the pastor. What about us? We can devote ourselves to secular work without distraction. But please remember, in Taoism the Taoist priests chant the liturgy for people; in Judaism the priests manage the things of God for men. However, in the church, there should not be any mediatorial class, because we ourselves are all priests.

It is for this reason that we have been crying out concerning the "universal priesthood" for twenty years. Abel could offer a sacrifice; so could Noah. In the beginning the people of Israel could all offer sacrifices; but later, because of the incident of the golden calf, they could not offer sacrifices themselves. God says that every believer can come directly to God. But now there are the mediatorial people in the church. Today there are Nicolaitans in the church; therefore, Christianity has become Judaism. The Lord is pleased with those who reject the mediatorial class. If you have been washed by the blood, you have a direct share in spiritual affairs. The church can only be founded on this ground; otherwise, it is Judaism. Therefore, we are not just fighting the matter of sects, but we are fighting for the privilege of the blood. Today there are three main categories of churches in the world: one is the world church, that is, the Roman Catholic Church; one is the state church, such as the Anglican Church and the Lutheran Church; and one is the independent church, such as the Methodist Church, the Presbyterian Church, etc. In the Roman Catholic Church there is the (Catholic) priestly system, in the Anglican Church there is the clerical system, and in the independent churches there is the pastoral system. All we see is a mediatorial class which undertakes spiritual affairs. But the church God wants to establish is one in which He can place the whole gospel without the mediatorial class. If there is anything present that does not conform to the whole gospel, then that is not the church.

"He who has an ear, let him hear what the Spirit says to the churches" (Rev. 2:7a). The Lord speaks in this same way to all the seven churches, showing that not only the church at Ephesus should hear, but all the churches must hear.

"To him who overcomes, to him I will give to eat of the tree of life, which is in the Paradise of God" (v. 7b). God's original intention for man was that he eat of the fruit of the tree of life. Now God says that we can come directly to Him and do according to His original intention. The question is not what the tree of life is; rather, the question is whether we are willing to follow God's initial intention to eat of the fruit of the tree of life in the garden of God. Only the overcomers can eat. Whoever returns to the original intention and demand of God is an overcomer.

CHAPTER THREE

THE CHURCH IN SMYRNA

Scripture Reading: Rev. 2:8-11

Now we continue by looking at the second church, the church in Smyrna. May God open our eyes that we may see more and neglect nothing. In the history of the church, the churches during the apostolic age and immediately after were greatly persecuted. Suffering is the special feature of the church; therefore, the name of the church here is Smyrna. Smyrna comes from the word *myrrh;* thus it means suffering and represents the church under persecution.

This epistle reveals that the name of the Lord Jesus is special and that the reward for the overcomer is also special. The Lord Jesus speaks of Himself as *"the First and the Last, who became dead and lived again"* (Rev. 2:8). To the overcomer the Lord says that he *"shall by no means be hurt of the second death"* (v. 11). This proves that life overcomes death. Many people have only seen "living," but they have not seen "living forever and ever" (1:18); neither have they seen "lived again" (2:8). How great this is! On the day of Pentecost the apostle said to the people, "Whom God has raised up, having loosed the pangs of death, since it was not possible for Him to be held by it" (Acts 2:24). Death cannot hold Him. Once all those who are alive go into death, they cannot come out again, but the Lord Jesus cannot be held by death. Death has no strength to hold Him. This is resurrection. His life can endure death; therefore, the principle of resurrection in the Bible becomes very precious. *"Who became dead and lived again"* proves that life can endure death. God sees the church as a being that can endure death. The gates of Hades are open to the church, but the gates of Hades cannot prevail against her and cannot confine her; thus, the nature of the church is resurrection. Whenever the church loses her power to overcome suffering, she is useless. Many people are finished upon encountering certain matters contrary to their wishes; for them it is just like encountering death. But resurrection does not fear death; suffering only proves that one can endure death. You may think that a certain man will probably be finished after encountering a certain incident, but, no, he passes through and comes out again. That which passes through death and still remains is resurrection.

Even in our own lives, there are many occasions like this. When we encounter trials and temptations, prayer may cease and it may become difficult to read the Word. The brothers all say that this time we are finished, but not long after, we rise, and the life of God comes forth from us again. That which is finished after death is not resurrection. The church has a basic principle: She is able to pass through death; she cannot be buried. The church in Smyrna especially expresses this truth. If you read the history of martyrdom by Fox, you will see how the church has suffered persecutions and afflictions.

For example, Polycarp was a bishop of the church at that time, and he was seized by his opponents. Since he was eighty-six years old, they could not bear to put him to death, and they were especially lenient towards him. He only needed to say, "I do not recognize Jesus of Nazareth," and they would have set him free. But he replied, "I cannot deny Him. I have been serving Him for eighty-six years, and in these eighty-six years He has never treated me wrongly. How can I deny Him for the love of my body!" As a result, they carried him to the fire and burned him. While the lower half of his body was withering in the flames, he still could say, "Thank God that I have the opportunity today to be burned by men and to give my life to testify for You."

There was a sister who was told that if she would only bow to Diana (the idol Artemis in the city of Ephesus, as recorded in Acts 19), she would be released. What did she say? She replied, "Do you ask me to choose between Christ and Diana? I chose Christ the first time, and now you want me to choose again. I still choose Christ." As a result she too was slain. Two sisters who were present said, "So many of God's children have been taken away. Why do we still remain?" Later, they too were taken and put into prison. These sisters witnessed many being devoured by beasts and they said again, "Many have testified with their blood. Why do we testify only with our mouth?" One of these sisters was married, and the other was engaged. Their parents, husband, and fiancé all came to persuade them otherwise. They even brought the child of the married sister, begging them to deny the Lord. But they said, "What can you bring that compares with Christ?" As a result they were dragged out and given to the lions to be devoured. The two sang as they walked until they were torn apart by the beasts.

How terrible were the persecutions suffered by the church in Smyrna! But no matter what happens, life always revives after it has died. Persecutions only manifest what kind of church the church is. He is "the First and the Last, who became dead and lived again."

"I know your tribulation and poverty" (Rev. 2:9). You have nothing founded on this earth, but the Lord knows that you are rich. *"Do not fear the things that you are about to suffer"* (v. 10). The entire church in Smyrna was persecuted, but the life which has died and is now living again can break through all these persecutions. The church in Smyrna was able to endure great persecutions because she knew resurrection. Only resurrection can bring us out of the grave.

"I know...the slander from those who call themselves Jews and are not" (v. 9). Here we must give heed to the problem of the Jews. The Lord said that the church has tribulation and poverty in her sufferings; these are easy to deal with. But that which comes from within is not easy to deal with. The Jews spoken of here do not refer to the Jews in the world but to the Jews in the church, just as the "people" we saw before in connection with the Nicolaitans did not refer to the people in the world but to the laity in the church. Here the Lord speaks of the Jews who persecuted them. This is the most painful among painful things. In the seven epistles there is a line of opposition. The Nicolaitans are spoken of twice—once to the church in Ephesus and once to the church in Pergamos.

The Jews are spoken of twice as well—once here and again to the church in Philadelphia. In the epistle to Pergamos, the teaching of Balaam is referred to, and in the epistle to Thyatira, Jezebel is referred to. All of these constitute the line of opposition. We may ask what the meaning of the Jews is. Is not salvation of the Jews? Why do they speak blasphemy here? For this reason we must know what Judaism is and what the church is.

There are many essential differences between Judaism and the church. Here I wish to mention four points to which we must give special attention: the temple, the law, the priests, and the promises. As their place of worship, the Jews built a splendid temple on this earth of stone and gold. As their standard of behavior, they have the Ten Commandments and many other regulations. In order to attend to spiritual affairs, they have the office of the priests, a group of special people. Finally, they also have the blessings by which they may prosper on this earth. Please notice that Judaism is an earthly religion on this earth. They have a material temple, regulations of letters, mediatorial priests, and enjoyment on this earth.

When the Jews entered the land of Canaan, they built the temple. If I am a Jew and want to serve God, I must go to the temple. If I feel I have sinned and need to offer a sacrifice, I must go to the temple to offer the sacrifice. If I feel God has blessed me and I wish to give thanks, I must go to the temple to give thanks. I must go this way all the time. I can only worship God when I get to the temple. This is called the place of worship. The Jews are worshippers, and the temple is the place where they worship. The worshippers and the place of worship are two different things. But is this so in the New Testament? The special feature of the church is that there is no place and no temple, because we, the people, are the temple.

Ephesians 2:21-22 says, "In whom all the building, being fitted together, is growing into a holy temple in the Lord; in whom you also are being built together into a dwelling place of God in spirit." Have you seen this? The special feature of the church is that your body is the dwelling place of God.

Individually speaking, every one of us is the temple of God. Corporately speaking, God builds us up and fits us together to become His dwelling place. There is no place of worship in the church; the place of worship is the worshipper. We carry our place of worship wherever we go. This is basically different from Judaism. The temple in Judaism is a material temple; the temple in the church is a spiritual temple. Someone once calculated the total value of the Jewish temple—it was enough to afford all the people in the world a monetary share. But what about the temple of Christians today? Some are crippled, some are blind, and some are poor, but this is the temple. Today some people say, "If you do not go to the solemn and magnificent temple, at least you need a 'church' building." But the church does not have a "church" building. Wherever the believers go, there the church building goes as well. God dwells in men, not in a house. In the church God dwells in man; in Judaism God dwells in a house. Man thinks that he needs a place in order to worship God. Some even call the building the "church." This is Judaism, not the church! The word *church* in Greek is *ekklesia,* which means "the called-out ones." The church is a people bought with the precious blood; this is the church. Today we can have the temple upstairs, we can have the temple at the porch of Solomon, we can have the temple at the gate called Beautiful, and we can have the temple downstairs. Judaism has the material place. Who then are the Jews? They are those who bring the material place into the church. If God's children wish to walk in His way, they must ask God to open their eyes so that they may see that the church is spiritual, not material.

The Jews also have laws and regulations for their daily life (God only uses the law to make men know their sins). Whoever is a Jew must keep the Ten Commandments. But the Lord Jesus says clearly that even if you have kept the Ten Commandments, you still lack one thing (Luke 18:20-22). Judaism has a standard of principles for daily living which is written on tablets of stone. These must be memorized. But there is a problem: If I am literate, I know them; if I am illiterate, I do not know them. If I have a good memory,

I can remember them; if I do not have a good memory, I cannot remember them. This is Judaism. The daily-living standard of Judaism is dead; it is something outward. In the church there is no law; rather, its law is in another place. It is not written on tablets of stone but on tablets of the heart. The law of the Spirit of life is within us. The Holy Spirit dwells in us; the Holy Spirit is our law. Read Hebrews 8 and Jeremiah 31. In Hebrews 8:10 God says, "I will impart My laws into their mind, and on their hearts I will inscribe them" (cf. Jer. 31:33). Right or wrong is not on tablets of stone but in the heart. Today our special feature is that the Spirit of God dwells in us.

I would like to recount a story which expresses this meaning. In Kuling there was a Mr. Yu, an electrician, who had very little schooling. Later, he was saved. When the days grew cold, he was about to drink wine according to his old habit. The meal was ready, the wine was warmed, and he, his wife, and an apprentice were all seated and ready to eat. He started to say grace; yet for some time no sound came forth. At length he said, "Now that I am a Christian, I wonder if it is right for Christians to drink wine. It is too bad Brother Nee has left; otherwise, we could ask him. Let us search the Bible to see if it is all right for Christians to drink wine." So the three of them began to turn the pages of the Bible, but they could find nothing. At last the wife suggested that they take it this time. Later, she said, they could write a letter to me, and if I replied that it is not right to drink, they would quit; if I replied that it is all right to drink, they could continue. So Brother Yu stood again and prepared to say grace. But again no sound came forth for a short while. After this incident I met him, and the matter was brought up. I asked if he actually drank at that time, and he replied, "The 'householder' who dwells within me would not allow me to do it; so I did not drink." There is a "householder"—this is a very good statement. If the Holy Spirit disagrees, whatever we may say avails nothing; if the Holy Spirit agrees, whatever we may say also avails nothing. The law becomes an inward matter, not an outward one.

There are written laws and regulations in Judaism. Today

there are also many written rules and regulations in the "church," but this is not the church. Any regulation that is set up outwardly is not the church. We do not have outward laws; our standard of daily living is inward. The tribulation of the church in Smyrna was due to the fact that those who called themselves Jews were imposing Judaistic regulations upon her. In Judaism the men who worship and the God who is worshipped are separated and far removed from each other. The distance is Judaism. When man sees the God of Judaism, he will immediately die. How can those in Judaism draw near to God? They must depend upon the priest as a mediator. The priests represent them to God. The people are secular; they can only do secular things and be worldly. But the priests should be entirely holy and attend to holy things. The responsibility of the Jews is to bring the ox or the sheep to the temple. As for the matter of serving God, that is the business of the priests, not the business of the Jews. But in the church it is not so. In the church God not only wants us to bring material things to Him. He also desires that we, the people, come to Him. Today the mediatorial class has been abolished. What were the words of blasphemy spoken by the Jews? Some in the church in Smyrna were saying, "There will be no order at all if the brothers can baptize people, if the brothers can break the bread, and if everything is given to the brothers to do! That would be terrible!" They wanted to establish a mediatorial class.

Today's Christianity has already been Judaized. Judaism has priests, but Christianity has strict fathers, clergymen who are not as strict, and ordinary pastors in the pastoral system. The fathers, clergymen, and pastors undertake the spiritual things for everyone. Their only expectation from the church members is a donation. We the laity (the common believers) are secular; we can only do secular things and be as worldly as we like. But, brothers and sisters, the church does not have any secular (worldly) people! This does not mean that we do not attend to any secular things, but that the world cannot touch us. In the church everyone is spiritual. Let me tell you, whenever the church comes to the point of having only a handful of people undertake the spiritual things, that church has already fallen. We all know that the Roman Catholic fathers are not allowed to marry, because the more they differ in appearance from human beings, the safer people will feel in entrusting them with spiritual things. The church is nothing like that. The church demands that we offer our whole body to God. This is the only way. Everyone must be serving the Lord. Doing secular things is only for the purpose of taking care of our daily needs.

We now proceed to the fourth point. The purpose of the Jews in serving God is that they may reap more wheat from the fields and that their oxen and sheep will not drop their young but multiply manyfold, just as in Jacob's case. They are after blessings in this world. God's promises to them are also promises of earth, that among the nations on earth they may be the head and not the tail. But the first promise to the church is that we must take up the cross and follow the Lord. Sometimes when I preach the gospel, men ask, "Will there be any rice to eat when we believe in Jesus?" I have replied, "When you believe in Jesus, the rice-bowl is broken." This is the church. It is not that we will gain more in everything after we believe. Once when I was in Nanking, a certain preacher said in his message, "If you only believe in Jesus, you may not make big money, but you will at least make a fair living." When I heard this, I thought that this was not according to the church. The church does not teach how much we shall gain before God, but how much we will be able to let go before God. The church does not think that suffering is a painful thing; rather, it is a joy. Today these four items—the material temple, the outward laws, the mediatorial priests, and the worldly promises—are in the church. Brothers and sisters, we desire to preach the word of God more. We hope that all the children of God, even though they have secular occupations, will be spiritual men.

In Revelation 2:9 the Lord speaks a very strong word: *"Those who call themselves Jews and are not, but are a synagogue of Satan."* The word "synagogue" is especially related to Judaism, just as "shrine" is related to Buddhism, "monastery" to Taoism, and "mosque" to Mohammedanism. A certain brother said that we should not call our meeting place a church assembly hall, but a Christian synagogue. If so, when a Jew passed by, he would greatly misunderstand; for *synagogue* is a term used exclusively in Judaism. How can we say that there is such a thing as a Christian synagogue and yet not bring in Judaism? The Lord says that they are the synagogue of Satan. The Jews spoken of here refer to the Jews in the church, because they even bring in a "synagogue." May God be merciful to us. We must utterly get rid of all the things of Judaism.

In the church in Smyrna there was tribulation, poverty, and the slander of the Jews. But what does the Lord say to them? *"Do not fear the things that you are about to suffer. Behold, the devil is about to cast some of you into prison that you may be tried"* (v. 10). Fear not! Many times if we could only know that something is caused by Satan, the problem would be half settled. It is when we start thinking that it is caused by men that we have difficulty. If we could only know that it is done by the enemy, the problem would be solved and our heart could immediately rest before the Lord.

"You will have tribulation for ten days" (v. 10). Here we have the problem of "ten days." Many expositors of Revelation and Daniel are accustomed to counting one day as a year. Since they count these ten days as ten years, they look for these ten years in history but find nothing. I personally feel that there is absolutely no scriptural basis for this. There are many places in the Bible where days cannot be reckoned as years. For example, Revelation 12:14 says, "A time and times and half a time," referring to three and a half years, and verse 6 speaks of "a thousand two hundred and sixty days." A Jewish calendar year is 360 days; therefore, 1,260 days are three and a half years. If one day is equivalent to one year, then this would become 1,260 years. If the great tribulation were to last for such a long time, what would people do?

What then is the actual meaning of ten days? In the Bible ten days are spoken of many times. In Genesis 24:55 there are "ten days." When the servant wanted to take Rebecca with him, Rebecca's brother and mother requested that she stay with them for at least ten days. When Daniel and his friends would not allow themselves to be defiled by the king's food, they asked the officer in charge to try them for ten days (Dan. 1:11-12). So "ten days" in the Bible has a meaning, that is, a very short time. The words which the Lord speaks here have the same meaning. On one hand, this means that there are certain days for our suffering, and that our days of suffering are counted by the Lord. After these days, we shall be released just as Job was. On the other hand, it means that the ten days are a very short time. No matter what trials we pass through before God, they will not last long. When the days are fulfilled, the devil can do nothing. The trials which we suffer will pass quickly.

"Be faithful unto death, and I will give you the crown of life" (Rev. 2:10). Faithful unto death is a matter both of time and of attitude. The Lord insists that the life of all those who serve Him belongs to Him. This is why we must be faithful even unto death. Whoever is bought with the precious blood belongs to the Lord and must be wholly for the Lord. From the very outset Christ demands our all. Now He says, "Be faithful unto death." As to our attitude, we must be faithful even unto death; as to time, we must be faithful until death. "I will give you the crown of life." The crown is a reward; at that time, life will become a crown.

"He who has an ear, let him hear what the Spirit says to the churches. He who overcomes shall by no means be hurt of the second death" (v. 11). Here it clearly says that not only will we escape the second death, but we will not suffer the hurt of this death, for we have already learned the lesson. Tribulations are severe; if we have not been in tribulations, we never know how terrible they are. Poverty is oppressive; if we have never been poor, we do not know the taste of it. Slander is also oppressive; if we have never been slandered, we do not know its painfulness. It is as if every encounter drags us into death, but as we pass through, we prove that resurrection is a fact. The Lord came out of the grave, and we too will come out. His resurrection life today cannot be drowned, so we dare to say that we too cannot be drowned.

CHAPTER FOUR

THE CHURCH IN PERGAMOS

Scripture Reading: Rev. 2:12-17

The church in Ephesus was the church at the end of the apostolic age, the church before the apostle John passed away, the church which John himself referred to as in the last time, and the church spoken of in 2 Peter and 2 Timothy. This we have seen. Then we saw in the preceding chapter, the age wherein the church was persecuted, which is the prophecy of the church in Smyrna as shown to us by the Lord. Now we will look at the church in Pergamos.

The name *Pergamos* means "marriage" or "union." Here we see how the church has taken a turn. I think the believers at that time, when they read concerning Pergamos, probably did not understand what this letter meant. But when we look back upon the history of the church it is quite clear. Gibbon, a historian, said that if they had killed all the Christians in the city of Rome, the city would have become uninhabited. The greatest persecution in the entire world was not able to destroy the church. Therefore, Satan changed his method of attack. The world not only ceased to oppose the church, but even the greatest empire on this earth—Rome—accepted Christianity as the state religion. It is said that Constantine had a dream in which he saw a cross with the words written on it, "By this sign conquer." He discovered that the cross was a sign of Christianity; so he accepted Christianity as the state religion. He encouraged people to be baptized, and whoever was baptized was given two white robes and a few pieces of silver. The church was united with the world; therefore, the church became fallen. In the previous chapter we read that the church of Smyrna was the church of suffering and that the Lord had nothing to say against her.

Here Pergamos and the world are united to become the biggest state religion. According to men, this would be an advancement; yet the Lord is displeased. When the church unites herself with the world, the testimony of the church is wrecked. The church is a sojourner in the world. It is all right for the boat to be on the water, but not for the water to be in the boat.

"He who has the sharp two-edged sword..." (Rev. 2:12). The Lord speaks of Himself as the One who has the sword with two edges. Here is judgment.

The church has fallen, but this does not mean that the church in that age had no testimony at all. No matter what circumstance she is in, the reality of the church is always there. Pergamos is the church which continues immediately after Smyrna. In what kind of situation is she? In verse 13 the Lord said, *"I know where you dwell, where Satan's throne is."* The Lord recognizes the difficulty of Pergamos's situation. Since she dwells in the very place of Satan's throne, it is rather difficult for her to maintain a testimony. Here is a person who is very special, that is, "Antipas, My witness, My faithful one, who was killed among you." We cannot find his name in history; therefore, since this is a prophecy, we must discover the meaning from the name itself. *Anti* means "against"; *pas* means "all." Antipas is a faithful man who is against all; he opposes all things. This does not mean that he intentionally creates troubles regardless of the situation, but that he stands on the side of God to oppose all things. Of course, this person must become a martyr. History does not know his name, but the Lord knows.

Regarding this faithful man who is slain, in verse 13 the Lord said, *"You hold fast My name and have not denied My faith."* Two matters are mentioned: the Lord's name and the Lord's faith. The children of God are those whom God has chosen out from among the Gentiles unto the name of the Lord. There is a basic difference between the church and religion. In religion it is sufficient to accept teachings, but in the church it is meaningless if one does not believe in the Lord. The name of the Lord represents the Lord Himself. This is a special feature. Not only so, this name also tells us that He has been here and has gone back, He died and lives again; therefore, He leaves a name in our midst. If we lose the name of our Lord, we no longer have the testimony. Pergamos receives the name of the Lord. There is one thing to which the children of God must especially take heed: We must manifest ourselves as those who are in the name of the Lord. This name is a special name, a name which will keep us from losing the testimony.

He also said, *"You...have not denied My faith."* The word "faith" here in Greek is *pistin.* The meaning of this word is "belief." It is not an ordinary belief, but the unique belief, the belief which is distinct from all other beliefs. The Lord said that Pergamos had not denied His unique faith. The church is not something of philosophy, natural science, ethics, or psychology. These are not things of the church. The church is something of belief, something of faith. *"You...have not denied My faith."* What does this mean? This means, "You have not denied believing in Me." The children of God must maintain this belief. Our belief in the Lord Jesus must not change at all. This faith is what separates us from the world. So *"You hold fast My name and have not denied My faith"*—these two points are the things for which the Lord praised her.

"But I have a few things against you, that you have some there who hold the teaching of Balaam, who taught Balak to put a stumbling block before the sons of Israel, to eat idol sacrifices and to commit fornication" (v. 14). Balaam was a Gentile; we do not know why God also called him a prophet. As in the case of Saul, the Spirit of God moved him but did not enter into him. Because the people of Israel were continually victorious, Balak was afraid and called for Balaam. He said to him, "You are a prophet. Please curse the people of Israel." Balaam coveted the money offered to him and was desirous to go, and though God hindered him at first, He later permitted him. But Balaam could find no way to curse the people of Israel. Since he had accepted Balak's money and had done nothing in return, he felt uncomfortable. Therefore, he conceived a scheme in which the Moabite women would draw near to the people of Israel. The people of Israel took

these Moabite women and were united with them. These Gentile women also brought their idols with them, causing the people of Israel not only to commit fornication but also to worship idols. God was angry and slew 24,000 Israelites, but Moab was preserved. In Numbers 25, we see that the Moabite women were united with the Israelites, but it is not until chapter thirty-one that we discover the scheme was designed by Balaam.

God shows us what Pergamos is: The meaning of Pergamos is marriage to the world. Originally, the world opposed the church; now the world and the church are married. I have said many times that the meaning of the "church" *(ekklesia)* is the called-out ones; not united, not placed in the world, but separated, called out—this is the church. The method of Balaam is to destroy the separation between the church and the world, and the result is idol worship.

Here we must pay special attention to two things—fornication and idol worship. It is very strange that these two are put together. In 1 Corinthians these two matters are also mentioned together. In the flesh these are the two things which God hates, and in spiritual things these are also the two things which God hates. Hear what James 4:4 says about this: "Do you not know that the friendship of the world is enmity with God?" To be united with the world is what God hates. Mammon also stands in opposition to God. "You cannot serve God and mammon" (Matt. 6:24). Men either serve one or the other. Here we see a most important matter: Mammon stands against God. Many idols exist only because of mammon. Today no Christian would kill people or worship idols, but if we covet money and trust in the power of mammon, it is equivalent to idol worship. Mammon is the principle of idols, and God desires to separate men from mammon. Fornication is connected with idol worship, and coveting money is connected with union with the world. I like to place the opposite sides in the Bible before you. If you can see the negative side, then you can see the positive side. The Bible always puts Satan in opposition to Christ, the flesh in opposition to the Holy Spirit, and the world and mammon in opposition to God the Father. The world is opposed to the

Father. According to 1 John 2:15, "If anyone loves the world, love for the Father is not in him." Mammon stands against God. Whenever man serves mammon, he cannot serve God. The work of Balaam is to unite the world with the church. The need for Constantine to exalt us is the teaching of Balaam. Nothing is more difficult than keeping the work of Balaam from getting in. Today the children of God all want to be great, to have more, and to pay no attention to holiness and cleanliness. Thus, they yield to sins, they yield to the teaching of Balaam, and they allow the Lord's name to be denied.

The Lord specifically mentions Balaam in this epistle. Balaam was the first to make money from his gifts. There are several passages in the New Testament which speak of Balaam. Second Peter 2:15 says that Balaam "loved the wages of unrighteousness." Jude 11 indicates that Balaam was one who was greedy for reward. Let us consider this. Do you think it would be possible for the church at Corinth to invite Paul and yet first discuss the matter of reward? Do you think the church in Jerusalem signed a contract with Peter for a certain amount of compensation every year? We absolutely cannot conceive of such things happening. Originally, those who worked for God depended upon God for their living; they asked nothing from man and they would not accept money from the Gentiles (3 John 7). But during the time of Constantine, all those who served God received salaries from the state treasury. It was a little after A.D. 300 when this practice began. When everyone received a salary, the method of Balaam came in. Balaam's method has no place in God's plans. If you asked the apostles how much salary they received each month, would this not be a joke? But today this condition has become commonplace. If we can trust in God, then we go to work; if we cannot trust in God, then we do not go to work. We must pay special attention to this matter before the Lord.

Immediately following Revelation 2:14, the Nicolaitans are mentioned again. "In the same way..."—these words especially form a link with the preceding words. The Lord shows His disapproval of the teaching of Balaam; in the same way the

Lord disapproves of the teaching of the Nicolaitans. In the Bible God Himself has ordained what the church should be like. Read Matthew 20:25-28: "But Jesus called them to Him and said, You know that the rulers of the Gentiles lord it over them, and the great exercise authority over them. It shall not be so among you; but whoever wants to become great among you shall be your servant, and whoever wants to be first among you shall be your slave; just as the Son of Man did not come to be served, but to serve and to give His life as a ransom for many." Do you see? The church is established by the Lord; a class of princes and those who are great is not permitted. The Lord said that whoever wants to be great among you shall be your servant; whoever is the servant is the chief. Greatness is not decided on the basis of position, but on the basis of service. If you look into Matthew 23:8-11, it is even more evident. The basic principle of the church is: All are brothers; there are no rabbis, no instructors, no fathers.

When Constantine accepted Christianity, the teaching of Balaam occurred and the teaching of the Nicolaitans appeared. We see here the system of the fathers. Among the many fathers, the one who stands above them all is the pope. When anyone kisses his feet, he must cry, "My Lord." At the same time there are high officials in the Vatican, and many countries are represented by ambassadors and ministers. There are kings and high officials; there are those who are called father and those who are called rabbi. This is the teaching of the Nicolaitans which we have seen. Those who have position and reputation in the world must be careful not to bring the things of the world into the church. If you cannot call the humble one who sits beside you a brother, something is wrong with you. When you are sitting among the brothers and sisters, and yet you cannot be a brother or sister, then the Nicolaitans appear. The word *laos* in the original Greek word *nikaolaos* not only means laity (common people), but it also means laymen in contrast with experts and specialists. For example, the medical doctors are specialists, and those who are not are called laymen. When a carpenter meets another carpenter, they are of the same trade and both experts. When he meets one who is not a carpenter, he calls him a layman or one who is outside the trade. *Nicolait* means to conquer the laymen, indicating that there is a group of people who are experts, that is, men inside the trade, while the rest are laymen, that is, men outside the trade. The Lord says that this is what He is "against."

The condition of the church in Ephesus and that of the church in Pergamos are different. The church in Ephesus only has the behavior of the Nicolaitans, while the church in Pergamos has the teaching of the Nicolaitans. It takes some time for behavior to become a teaching. If a certain behavior is manifested and then a doctrine is preached, this involves not only the ability to behave, but also the ability to produce a theory based on that behavior. This is a further step. Behavior comes before teaching. When teaching appears, that is quite serious. Several years ago I met a church member who took a concubine. Someone asked me to advise him. Not only did he think that it was all right to take a concubine, but he also brought out examples in the Bible to cover his sin. Taking a concubine is behavior; quoting the Bible becomes a teaching. So likewise today, there is the open teaching of the Nicolaitans. How did Pergamos form this teaching? We have already said that after Constantine accepted Christianity as the state religion, the church became married to the world. As long as one was a Roman, he could be baptized; hence, the church was filled with unbelievers. Originally, only brothers were in the church, and all the brothers were priests. Then a mixed multitude came in. To ask them to serve God was impossible. For convenience sake then, they chose a group of people, saying, "You attend to the spiritual matters; the others can still be the common people, the laymen." Many of those who became church members did not know the Lord Jesus at all; therefore, those who knew the Lord Jesus became the experts. As a result, the Nicolaitans appeared. This is the inevitable result of a marriage between the church and the world. What the Nicolaitans did was only a kind of behavior in Ephesus, but in Pergamos it became a kind of teaching. Thereafter, the church became the business of the experts, not the laymen. It became a teaching that it is all right for men not to be spiritual, that spiritual affairs can be entrusted to the care of the experts, and that the common people may just attend to secular affairs. It became a doctrine that there are two kinds of people in the church: Those who undertake spiritual affairs and those who take care of secular things. For the ordinary, common people, it is enough just to attend the meetings; they need not care about other things. If someone tried to bring in the principles of meeting in 1 Corinthians 14, it would not work. The doctrine of Balaam brought in the teaching of the Nicolaitans.

I believe this matter is what the Lord hates the most; therefore, we have to pay special attention to it. I recognize the matter of the ministry. I also acknowledge that Paul engaged in tent-making at the same time, and also that Peter, James, and John devoted themselves entirely to preaching. But today what we call the position of the brothers is not related to the position of the ministry. In the local church, the brothers of the locality should be the deacons and the elders. All the brothers and sisters should take care of spiritual matters; they are the priests. The elders should not do everything for them; the elders only "oversee." As for the workers, when they come to the church, they have only the position of a brother. This is where the difference between the Nicolaitans and the brothers lies. The Bible shows us that all the children of the Lord testify, but the apostles testify more. The difference is a matter of degree, not of nature. The nature is identical; only the degree is different. But the teaching of the Nicolaitans changes this—spiritual affairs are taken care of by a special class. This is rebuked by God, for if this is the case, the church may be worldly and content just to have a few spiritual deacons. Several especially spiritual people will be selected from the church to take care of the spiritual affairs. They will become another class to undertake all the spiritual things. The system of fathers of the world church, the clergy system of the state church, and the pastoral system of the independent churches are all the same in nature. They are all Nicolaitans. In the Bible there are only brothers. There is the gift of a pastor, but no system of pastors. The pastoral system is man's tradition. If the children of God are not willing to return to the position of that in the beginning, no matter what they do, it will not be right. The church must not unite with the world and must not receive unbelievers into the church. Otherwise, it will be easy to accept the teaching of the Nicolaitans. People must be separated from the world before they can be brought into the church. Whenever we allow an unbeliever to come into the church, the church is no longer the church, but the world. The holiness and separation of the church must be maintained at any cost.

"Repent therefore; but if not, I am coming to you quickly, and I will make war with them with the sword of My mouth" (Rev. 2:16). Here the Lord speaks very strong words. If they will not repent, He will punish them with the sword of His mouth—that is, He will punish and judge those who rebel against Him. We pray God that there will be no Nicolaitans among us! I feel that if the church is spiritual, then Nicolaitans cannot be produced. Once the church becomes worldly, the Nicolaitans appear. God's requirement in the beginning for the people of Israel was that the whole nation be priests. God separated the Levites to be priests because the people of Israel sinned. When the church became worldly, the matter of serving God was committed to a few people. Now God wants all the people in the church to do the spiritual things.

"He who has an ear, let him hear what the Spirit says to the churches. To him who overcomes, to him I will give of the hidden manna, and to him I will give a white stone, and upon the stone a new name written, which no one knows except he who receives it" (v. 17). Two things are promised to the overcomer—the hidden manna and the white stone. The hidden manna and the manna in the wilderness are two different things. When the people of Israel were in the wilderness, manna came down from heaven daily for them to eat. Then Moses told them to take a golden pot, fill it with an omer of manna, and keep it in the ark. When later generations would ask about the matter, they could tell them how God sent down manna from heaven to feed them while they were in the wilderness. They had the manna in the ark as evidence (Exo. 16:14-35). Those of later generations who did not know what manna was could be shown the manna in

the ark. Then they would know. But those who had eaten of the manna would have another feeling towards the hidden manna. They had known the taste; thus, when they saw it again, they would have a kind of recollection. Those who had not tasted it would not have such a recollection, even though they knew what it was. To him who overcomes, the Lord will give to eat of the hidden manna. This means they will have recollections.

All our experiences before God are valuable and will not be lost. Many brothers ask me whether what they have passed through before God will be of any use in eternity. If you know the meaning of the hidden manna, you will know whether or not these will be of any use. If we have the opportunity to see the "hidden manna," then we will be able to review the "daily manna" once more. Whatever difficulty we go through and whatever tears we shed today will become our review. To me the hidden manna is the daily manna. Those who have never seen the manna will not have any recollection of it when they see the hidden manna on that day. Although they know the leading of His grace, they have not eaten of it. But those who have eaten of it will be full of recollections. The hidden manna is a very great principle in the Bible and also a great treasure. One day we shall eat of the heavenly, hidden manna. If we do not have any scars here, we are not over-comers. If we have never passed through things here, there will be no recollections or retasting of experiences in the future, even if we are given the hidden manna. Never say that what we encounter today is meaningless. No experience is a lost experience. On that day we all will be able to recall our experiences. We must not say that everything in the kingdom is the same. No, it is not the same! Our experience on this earth is related to what we will enjoy in that day. The hidden manna is known to those who know and unknown to those who do not know. Today we pass through hardships and tribulations, but on that day the Lord will wipe away our tears. How can those who have no tears know the preciousness of the wiping away of tears?

There is another reward, that is, the white stone, and the overcomer's new name is written upon the stone. The Lord gives him a new name which corresponds with his condition before the Lord. A brother wants me to change his name for him, but I do not know whether the name will need to be changed again after I have changed it. The Lord writes the name on the white stone; only the Lord and you will know it. The overcomer does not receive a special name; rather, he receives the name which he deserves. I hope that the Lord will open our eyes that we may know the way of the overcomer and that we may receive the hidden manna and the new name.

CHAPTER FIVE

THE CHURCH IN THYATIRA

Scripture Reading: Rev. 2:18-29

Now we will continue by looking at Thyatira. Here I must especially emphasize that Ephesus came forth after the church in the apostolic age had passed away, and after Ephesus, Smyrna, and after Smyrna, Pergamos, and after Pergamos, Thyatira. The church during the apostles' time has passed, the age of Ephesus has passed, the age of sufferings has passed, and the period of Pergamos has also passed. Although Thyatira follows, the church in Thyatira will continue until the Lord Jesus comes back again. Not only Thyatira, but also Sardis, Philadelphia, and Laodicea will continue until the Lord Jesus returns. In the first three churches there was no mention of the Lord's coming again, but in the latter four, the coming back of the Lord Jesus is spoken of in each case. Laodicea, however, does not speak of the Lord's second coming literally because of something particular concerning her, which we will explain later. The latter four churches will continue until the Lord Jesus comes again.

In the Bible the number seven signifies completeness. Seven is composed of three plus four. Three is the number of God; God Himself is three in one. Four is the number of the creature of God; it is the number of the world, including the four directions, the four winds, the four seasons, etc. All of these contain the number four. Seven means the Creator plus the creature. When God is added to man, that is completion. (But this completeness is of this world—God never puts seven in eternity. The number of completeness in eternity is twelve. Seven is three plus four; twelve is three times four. When God and man are put together, that is completeness in this world. When the Creator and the creature are joined together, then there is eternal completeness.) The number seven is always three plus four. The seven churches are divided into the first three churches and the last four. Three do not speak of the Lord's coming back, while the other four refer to the Lord's coming again. Thus, three churches belong to one group, while the other four belong to another group. The church in Thyatira is first among the four churches which will exist until the Lord Jesus comes again.

Thyatira means "the sacrifice of perfume," that is, full of many sacrifices. The words spoken by the Lord in this epistle become stronger and stronger. The Lord says that He is the One who has *"eyes like a flame of fire"* (Rev. 2:18). Nothing can hide from His eyes. He is the light; He Himself is the illumination. At the same time He says that *"His feet are like shining bronze"* (v. 18). In the Bible bronze signifies judgment. What the eyes see, the feet judge. All Bible scholars agree that the church in Thyatira refers to the Roman Catholic Church. This does not refer to the confusion which resulted from the marriage with the world in the beginning—that is now over. Now the situation has become so gross, so full of heresy and sacrifice. It is indeed remarkable how the Roman Catholic Church pays so much attention to behavior and sacrifice. The mass is their sacrifice.

The Roman Catholic Church, according to our observation, has nothing good, but God says, *"I know your works and love and faith and service and your endurance and that your last works are more than the first"* (v. 19). The Lord acknowledges that there is reality in the Roman Catholic Church. Madame Guyon, Tauler, and Fenelon were all in the Roman Catholic Church, and we can mention many more of the best names. Indeed, there are many in the Roman Catholic Church who know the Lord. We should never think that there are none who are saved in the Roman Catholic Church. The Lord still has His own people there—of this we must be very clear before the Lord.

What we are taking note of now is how desolate the church has become in her outward appearance. First, we saw the behavior of the Nicolaitans; later, we saw that it developed into a teaching. But what about the church now? The Lord says, *"But I have something against you, that you tolerate the woman Jezebel, she who calls herself a prophetess and teaches and leads My slaves astray to commit fornication and to eat idol sacrifices"* (v. 20). Who is Jezebel? Jezebel was the wife of Ahab, who married her from the land of the Zidonians, the Gentiles. Jezebel seduced the people to worship Baal (1 Kings 16:30-32). Baal was the god of the Gentiles, not the God of the people of Israel. Jezebel told the people to worship the image of Baal. The problem was not just idols, but that God had been replaced. Baal was brought in and worshipped as their own god. In the history of the Jewish nation (Israel) up to 1 Kings 16, no one had ever led the people of Israel to sin in such a way as Ahab. Ahab was the first to lead the people to worship a Gentile god on a large scale. Not even Jeroboam could match him in the sins he committed.

Here we want to note who Jezebel is. Jezebel is a woman. The woman in Revelation 17 refers to the Roman Catholic Church. In Matthew 13:33 the woman who took the leaven and hid it in three measures of meal is also the Roman Catholic Church. Naturally, therefore, the woman in Revelation 2:20 also represents the Roman Catholic Church.

God never acknowledges the marriage between His people and the Gentiles as proper; God says that this is fornication. So Jezebel was not the queen; the coming together of Ahab and Jezebel was fornication. Fornication is confusion. What God sees is a woman who is confusing the words of God and the people of God. This woman brought in the god of the Gentiles. I have already said that the result of fornication is idolatry. The New Testament speaks of the conference at Jerusalem, the result of which was to exhort the Gentile brothers to abstain from meat offered to idols and from fornication (Acts 15:29). Here we see that the fornication of Jezebel brought idols into the kingdom of Israel.

Through Jezebel, Ahab was joined to the world. No matter where you are, it is apparent that the Roman Catholic Church unites herself with political powers. She sends out ambassadors and ministers to various nations, and in important world crises she stands up to speak. The uniting of the church with the world is the Roman Catholic Church. They claim that their first pope was Peter. But I think Peter would say that he was a disciple of the poor Jesus of Nazareth; the glory and honor of the world had nothing to do with him. Yet the Roman Catholic Church maintains her position in the world and commands respect from the people. The practice of the Roman Catholic Church within these more than one thousand years is, according to the James 4:4, the same as the greatest adultery. Here we see that the church has lost her virginity. Today there is a group of people who think that they can bargain with others since they have such a large membership. According to men it is a type of advancement for the church to be able to bargain, but according to God, it is sin for the church to gain what the world has gained.

What is the result? Idolatry. The facts are placed before us; there is not one church that is like the Roman Catholic Church with so many idols. We can say that the best class of idols is made by the Roman Catholic Church. I stayed in the city of Rome for one month. During that time I continually felt one thing: If theirs is the church, then ours is not; if ours is, then theirs surely is not. There is no middle ground for the two to come together. The remarkable thing is that they have fulfilled what has been prophesied in the Bible. There is an image of the Father and an image of the Son; there are images of the apostles and images of the ancient saints. They worship Mary; they worship Peter. Jezebel teaches the Lord's servants to commit fornication and eat the meat offered to idols. Jezebel is spoken of because the church has brought in Gentile gods. We can see this in the book entitled *Mystery* by G. H. Pember. Catholicism takes in Gentile gods and hangs the signs of Christianity upon them. The most evident is the image of Mary. Some think that at least Mary is of Christianity. But the fact is that Greece has a goddess, India has a goddess, Egypt has a goddess, and China has a goddess; every religion in the world has a goddess, except Christianity. Since there must be a goddess, they bring forth Mary. Actually there is no goddess in Christianity—the origin of the concept of a goddess is the Gentiles. So this is idolatry on top of fornication. This is Jezebel bringing in the things of the Gentiles to the kingdom of Israel. She calls herself a prophetess because she wants to preach and to teach. The position of the church before God is that of a woman. Whenever the church has authority to preach, that is Jezebel. The church has nothing to say; in other words, the church has no word. The Son of God is the Word; therefore, only He has the word. Christ is the Head of the church; therefore, only He can speak. Whenever the church speaks, that is the preaching of the woman. The Roman Catholic Church is the woman preaching. In the Roman Catholic Church, what matters is what the church says, not what the Bible says or what the Lord says. It is quite remarkable that God says that Jezebel is the prophetess and the woman who speaks. "My slaves" refers to individual slaves. Jezebel has the authority to direct every believer. The people in the Roman Catholic Church do not read the Bible, because they are afraid of misunderstanding what God means. Only the fathers can understand and only the fathers can speak; therefore, only they can decide all matters. Basically the Roman Catholic Church is the preaching of the woman who decides what the children of God should do. Many doctrines have been changed because she speaks for the church and people must listen to the church. She pays attention to the thought that people must listen to the church and pope, not that people must listen to the Lord.

In church history there were persecutions by the Roman Empire, and there were also persecutions by the Roman Catholic Church. When the Roman Catholic Church in Spain persecuted the children of God, we do not know how many she killed. The punishment applied during the Inquisition was cruel to the extreme. After people were brought to the point of death, they were turned over to the government gasping for breath, in order to show that none were killed by them. She will always make you accept her doctrine. The Jewish nation (Israel) had only one woman who killed the prophets, Jezebel. In the previous centuries we do not know how many witnesses died at the hands of the Roman Catholic Church. They claim that what they decide is always right.

The people's ideas are entirely in their hands. The Lord said that the failure of Thyatira is due to the fact that she allows the teaching of Jezebel in her midst. *"And I gave her time that she might repent, and she is not willing to repent of her fornication"* (Rev. 2:21). They are still united with the world and filled with the behavior of the world. *"Behold, I cast her into a bed"* (v. 22)—not into a coffin, but into a bed. A coffin means it is finished; a bed means it is not finished. It means that she will not be changed throughout her entire life. The patient cannot be cured and cannot be changed. Continuing in her present condition, she is incurable—this is the condition of the Roman Catholic Church. In 1926 Mussolini and the pope signed an agreement, setting aside the Vatican from Italy so that it could become an independent state, having its own court and police, etc. Believers in the Roman Catholic Church increase yearly. In China there is not one newspaper published by a Protestant church, yet the Roman Catholic Church owns a paper. Their number exceeds the Protestants by three or fourfold. In Revelation 17 we see to what extent this church will develop. Now it is undoubtedly becoming stronger and stronger. But the Lord says to His own people, "Come out of her, My people" (18:4). What does the Lord say about those who have committed adultery with her and about her children? *"I cast...those who commit adultery with her, into great tribulation, unless they repent of her works; and her children I will kill with death"* (2:22-23). These words probably refer to God's destroying of the Roman Catholic Church through the Antichrist and his followers. *"And all the churches will know that I am He who searches the inward parts and the hearts; and I will give to each one of you according to your works"* (v. 23).

"But I say to you—the rest in Thyatira, as many as do not have this teaching, who have not known the deep things of Satan, as they say—I put no other burden upon you; nevertheless what you have hold fast until I come" (vv. 24-25). "The rest in Thyatira"; although Jezebel is here, there are still the rest. When Jezebel set out to kill Elijah, Elijah was greatly discouraged upon hearing it. What did he do? He hid

himself. Then God said to him, "What doest thou here?" While he was murmuring, the Lord said, "Yet I have left me seven thousand" (1 Kings 19:9-18). These are "the rest in Thyatira." When Jezebel lived on this earth, there was Elijah; in the Roman Catholic Church there have also been many who belonged to the Lord. Many were burned not only in Spain, but also in France and Great Britain. The blood of many was shed by the Roman Catholic Church. This is a fact. Today the Roman Catholic Church is still trying her best to persecute. Thank the Lord, there are still those who "do not have this teaching, who have not known the deep things of Satan, as they say." The phrase "deep things" in Greek is *bathea,* which means mystery. The Roman Catholic Church greatly likes to use this word. They have many mysteries or deep doctrines in their midst. These doctrines are not of the Lord, but are the words of Jezebel. The Lord will not put any other burden upon those who do not have this teaching, but they must hold fast to that which they already have. Hold fast "My works" which you have known—that is enough. Do not lose what you already have, "until I come."

"And he who overcomes and he who keeps My works until the end, to him I will give authority over the nations; and he will shepherd them with an iron rod, as vessels of pottery are broken in pieces, as I also have received from My Father" (Rev. 2:26-27). This is the first promise. What is the meaning of this? Everyone who tends sheep has a rod. When the sheep do not behave well, he can use the rod to beat them gently. Matthew 13:40-42 indicates that an angel will come and gather out of His kingdom all the things that offend, that is, use force to cast out all the things that are not right. But this does not mean that the nations will no longer exist in the millennium. We know they will still be there. Through the iron rod God will break these things into pieces.

God produces stones; man produces bricks. Bricks are very similar to stones. The tower of Babel was built of bricks. From the tower of Babel to 2 Timothy, all those who imitate Him are earthen vessels ("vessels of pottery"). The Lord says that the overcomer will shepherd the nations and break the earthen vessels in pieces. The word "shepherd" means that something is not accomplished all at once but rather done by beating one by one as the need arises. This is shepherding. This sort of thing will probably be done continuously until the new heaven and new earth are brought in. The kingdom is the introduction to the new heaven and new earth. In the new heaven and new earth, only righteousness dwells. That is why the iron rod must be used to shepherd the nations and break in pieces all the things that come out of men.

"And to him I will give the morning star" (Rev. 2:28). This is the second promise. The morning star is the so-called daybreak star in Chinese. At the darkest hour, just at the time the day is breaking, it appears for a little while, and then the sun arises. Many people see the sun, but few have seen the morning star. One day the Lord will be seen by the whole world, as recorded in Malachi 4:2: "The Sun of righteousness [will] arise." Before everyone sees the light, some may see it first while in darkness. This is what it means to receive the morning star. Just before the day breaks, it is really dark. But the morning star appears at that very moment. The Lord promises the overcomer that he will receive the morning star at the darkest time. This means that he will see the Lord and be raptured. When we see the sun, it is always during the daylight hours, but he who sees the morning star is one who makes a special point of rising to see while others are asleep. This is the promise to the overcomer.

"He who has an ear, let him hear what the Spirit says to the churches" (Rev. 2:29). The Lord is speaking not only to the Roman Catholic Church but also to all the churches.

In the first three epistles the calling to the overcomer comes after the phrase, "He who has an ear, let him hear." First there is "he who has an ear," and then there is the promise to the overcomer. But starting with Thyatira, the order is reversed. This proves that the first three churches are of one group, while the last four churches are of another. There is a difference between these two groups. Formerly, Smyrna came after the age of Ephesus had passed, and Pergamos came after Smyrna had passed, and Thyatira came after Pergamos had passed. But now Sardis comes even though Thyatira has not passed away. Thyatira will continue until the Lord comes back. Nor does Philadelphia come after Sardis has passed, nor does Laodicea appear after Philadelphia has passed. Rather, Sardis still exists when Philadelphia comes, and Philadelphia still exists when Laodicea appears. Thyatira, Sardis, Philadelphia, and Laodicea will continue until the Lord Jesus comes again. The first three all came and went, but the last four emerge gradually and continue together until the Lord comes back.

CHAPTER SIX

THE CHURCH IN SARDIS

Scripture Reading: Rev. 3:1-6

We have seen that during the time of the apostles there was the behavior of the Nicolaitans. After the behavior of the Nicolaitans, we have seen how Pergamos sinned greatly by bringing the world into the church. After the Nicolaitans came Jezebel, and at ·the same time idols were brought into the church. But there is a good point here: In Thyatira we see the judgment of Jezebel, the casting of her into a bed that she may not move; we also see that her followers will one day be killed. These prophecies have not yet been fulfilled; they will be fulfilled at the time of Babylon's fall in Revelation 17. The history of Thyatira began from the time Jezebel improperly brought idols into the church and will continue until she receives judgment. Now we must see one thing: When the church, in her continuous fall from the Nicolaitans, comes to the stage of Jezebel, God can no longer tolerate it. Then Sardis emerges. "Sardis" means "the remains." The church in Sardis is God's reaction to Thyatira. The history of revival in the churches throughout the entire world indicates divine reactions. Whenever the Lord begins a revival work, He is reacting. God's reaction is man's recovery. I would like you to keep this principle firmly in mind. Sardis appears because the Lord has seen the condition of Thyatira.

In Revelation several churches are in pairs. Sardis is connected with Ephesus. Philadelphia is connected with Smyrna, and Laodicea is connected with Pergamos. Only Thyatira stands alone. In Sardis the Lord says that His name is *"He who has the seven Spirits of God and the seven stars: I know your works, that you have a name that you are living, and yet you are dead"* (Rev. 3:1). The epistle to Ephesus says that

His right hand holds seven stars, while the epistle to Sardis says that He has the seven stars. Ephesus is the slackening after the apostles, that is, the changing from something good to bad; Sardis is the recovery from Thyatira, that is, the changing from something bad to good. Having works but no love is Ephesus; living in name but dead in reality is Sardis. So these two are a pair. The Lord manifests Himself as He who has the seven Spirits. The seven Spirits of God are sent of God to the world to work, and this refers to the work of life. The seven stars in Ephesus refer to the messengers; here they refer to the illumination. The work of recovery is half in the Spirit and half in the light.

Sardis is similar to Thyatira in that she includes a long period of time, from the reformed churches until the Lord comes back again. Although the time of Sardis is not as long as Thyatira, she refers not only to the church during the Reformation, but also to church history following the Reformation.

"*I know your works, that you have a name that you are living, and yet you are dead.*" I believe no one will doubt that Martin Luther was a servant of the Lord and the Reformation was the work of God. The Reformation was a great work, and it was a divine reaction. Surely the Lord used Luther as a mouthpiece; he was a man especially chosen by God. When Luther first started, the Reformation was entirely Sardis. His purpose was solely for recovery. The Lord does not say that the work of Luther was not good; rather, He says it was not complete. It was good, but not good enough. In the eyes of the Lord, He has not found anything complete—everything was a beginning without an end. The Lord is a Lord of completion; therefore, He requires completion. For this reason, we must ask Him that we may see.

The problem of justification was solved following Luther. Justification is by faith, and having peace before the Lord is by faith. Luther not only gave us justification by faith; he also gave us an open Bible. In Thyatira the authority is in the hands of Jezebel—in other words, in the hands of the church. It is a matter of what the church says, not what the Lord says. It is all a matter of what the mother church says:

All the people of the Roman Catholic Church listen to the mother church. So the Lord says He will kill her "children." You say the mother, but the Lord says the children. Luther showed us what the Lord says and what the Bible says. Men can read God's Word, and men can see for themselves what God actually says, not what Rome says. When the open Bible comes, the whole church is enlightened.

However, a problem arises: Protestantism did not give us a proper church. As a result, wherever the doctrine of justification by faith and the open Bible went, a state church was established. The Lutheran sect became the state church in many countries. Later, in England the Anglican Church came into being, which is also a state church. Beginning with Rome, the nature of the church was changed. By the time of justification by faith and the return of the open Bible, the Protestant churches had not yet seen what the church should be. Although there were justification by faith and the open Bible, the Protestant churches still followed the example of Rome and did not return to the church in the beginning. During the Reformation the problem of the church was not solved. Luther did not reform the church. Luther himself said that we should not think "justification by faith" is enough; there are many more things to be changed. Yet the people in the Protestant churches stopped right there. Luther did not stop, but they stopped and said that it was good enough. Although they went back to the faith of the beginning, the church herself remained unchanged. Formerly, there was the international church of Rome; now it is the state church of England or the state church of Germany—that is all.

Brothers, do you see? The Reformation did not bring the church back to the condition of the beginning; it only caused the world church to become state churches. Thyatira is condemned for putting the church in the world; likewise, Sardis is condemned for putting the church in the states. *"You have a name that you are living, and yet you are dead."* The Reformation was living, but there were still many dead things.

Later, many "dissenters" developed, such as the Presbyterian Church, etc. On one hand, there is the Roman Catholic Church; on the other hand, there are the Protestant churches. Among the Protestant churches, aside from those established according to states, there are also churches set up according to different opinions and doctrines. The dissenters do not take the state as the boundary but their doctrine as the boundary. Therefore, there are two kinds of churches among the Protestant churches: one is state and the other is private. Today we see the union of the state and the church in Germany, Great Britain, and so forth. Rome has the world church, while Great Britain and Germany, etc., have the state church. The kings and chiefs of the states do not want to listen to the pope, yet they want others to listen to them. In politics they want to be the kings; in religion they also want to be the kings. As a result, the state churches came into existence. People never raised the question as to what the church is like in the Bible. People did not go back to the Bible to see whether it is proper to have state churches. Later, the private churches came into being also. The establishment of the private churches was due to the exalting of a certain doctrine; thus, they separated themselves from those who did not have the same doctrine. The Baptist Church was established because someone saw baptism; the Presbyterian Church was established because someone saw the presbytery system in the church. The church was established not because someone knew what the church is; rather, the church was established according to a system. These two kinds of Protestant churches—the state and the private—the Lord says, have not gone back to the purpose in the beginning. This statement is most significant.

"Become watchful and establish the things which remain, which were about to die" (v. 2). This refers to justification by faith and the open Bible and the life that is gained from them. In the whole history of Sardis, these were about to die; therefore, the Lord said, "Establish the things which remain, which were about to die." Today in the Protestant churches, the regulations of men are still in force, even though the Bible is already opened. Therefore, the Lord said, *"I have found none of your works completed before My God"* (v. 2). Even

what they already have is not complete. Some of their things are not complete; they were not complete from the very start. *"Remember therefore how you have received and heard, and keep it and repent"* (v. 3).

Does the history of the Protestant churches end this way? No! The history of the Protestant churches is a history of revivals. When Luther first started, many were saved, revived, and greatly recovered. One characteristic of the Protestant churches is "recovery." We do not know to what extent the Holy Spirit will work. Luther reformed something; thus, the Lutheran Church came out. The truth of the presbytery was seen; thus, the Presbyterian Church was organized. Wesley appeared; therefore, the Methodist Church was established. Today in the world there are still many smaller churches. In 1914 there were already more than 1500 churches.

Thank the Lord, Sardis was often blessed by God. But once there was the blessing of the Lord, men organized something to contain the blessing. Although the Lord's blessing is still there, the sphere remains only that big. The Protestant churches are like a cup. At the beginning of revival, people will go wherever there is living water. Wherever the Spirit of God is moving, people will go in that direction. Men used a cup with the hope of preserving the living water without loss. The advantage of doing this is that it keeps the grace, and the disadvantage is that there is just one cup of blessing. In the first generation the cup was full. By the second generation the cup was only half filled, and the nebulousness began. By the third or fifth generation, the water was gone and only an empty cup was left. Then they began to argue with other denominations as to whose cup was better, though all the cups were worthless for drinking. What was the result? God reacted again, and in came another Sardis. This is the whole history of revival. When the grace of God comes, men immediately set up an organization to keep it. The organization remains, but the content is lost. However, the cup cannot be broken; there are always those who are zealous to maintain the cup continuously. Here is a matter of principle: The students of Wesley could never be equal to Wesley, nor could the students of Calvin match Calvin. The schools of the prophets seldom produced prophets—all the great prophets were chosen by God from the wilderness. The Spirit of God descends upon whomsoever He will. He is the Head of the church, not we. Men always think the living water is valuable and must be kept by organization, but it gradually declines through the generations until it completely dries up. After it dries up, the Lord gives us living water again in the wilderness.

On one hand, there is revival—praise the Lord! On the other hand, it must be rebuked before the Lord because it is never returned to the beginning. The Protestant churches have revivals continuously, but the Lord says they are not perfect, they have not gone back to the beginning. We must remember what was in the beginning. The problem is not how we receive and hear now; the problem is how we received and heard in the beginning. In Acts 2 many were saved, and the Lord said they continued steadfastly in the teaching and fellowship of the apostles, in the breaking of bread and the prayers. It does not say that they continued in the apostles' breaking of bread and the prayers, but in the teaching and fellowship of the apostles. The fellowship of Christ is the fellowship of the apostles; the teaching of Christ is the teaching of the apostles. God only counts the fellowship of the apostles as fellowship; He only counts the teaching of the apostles as teaching. We cannot invent a fellowship; neither can we invent a teaching. The mistake of Thyatira was that she manufactured her own teaching, since Jezebel was there. God does not want us to invent; He just wants us to receive. In the twentieth century anything can be invented, but not the teaching. In the Spirit we may talk about discovery, but in teaching there cannot be any invention. We must examine what we have received, what we have heard, and hold fast and repent.

"I will come as a thief, and you shall by no means know at what hour I will come upon you" (v. 3). "Come" is to come by descending. "Upon" in Greek is *epi*, which means I will descend by your side, not come upon you, but apart from you. The coming of the thief is a coming of *epi*. We are here, and he prowls up by our side. The Lord's use of words is very ingenious. We can translate it as, "I will come and pass by you, yet you will not know it."

The thief does not come to steal the cheap things; he always steals the best. The Lord will also steal the best from the earth. The best are in His hands, not outside of Him. We are in the house: one will be raptured, and one will be left. So the Lord says that if you will not watch, He will come. The Lord Jesus is coming back soon. The day is getting closer. May we be precious enough to be "stolen" by the Lord.

"*But you have a few names in Sardis who have not defiled their garments, and they will walk with Me in white because they are worthy*" (v. 4). Jacob brought seventy souls into Egypt (Exo. 1:5). Ordinarily the Scriptures say so many men, so many souls. But the Lord says here that there are a few names; the Lord pays special attention to our names. He says that there are a few names who have not defiled their garments. These garments are our righteous deeds. When we stand before God, we put on Christ, for Christ is our white garment. However, we are not standing before God here, but before Christ, before the judgment seat (Rom. 14:10). We do not put on Christ here; rather, we put on "fine linen, bright and clean; for the fine linen is the righteousnesses of the saints" (Rev. 19:8). There are a few names which have not defiled their garments; that is to say, their behavior is clean. They will walk with the Lord, for they are worthy.

"*He who overcomes will be clothed thus, in white garments, and I shall by no means erase his name out of the book of life, and I will confess his name before My Father and before His angels*" (3:5). The matter here does not involve whether the name is recorded, but whether the name will be confessed. Those whom the Lord confesses will participate in something; those whom the Lord does not confess will not participate. All the names are recorded in the book of life, but he who is not confessed by the Lord is like one who is marked out with a circle. He will not participate. Here the problem is not related to eternal life in eternity, but to whether or not you can reign with the Lord. It is an unfortunate thing to be recorded and yet not be able to participate. May the Lord be gracious to us so that we may wear the white garment before the Lord. We have the white garment to put on before God, but what about before the Lord?

A SYSTEMATIC CHART OF CHURCH HISTORY

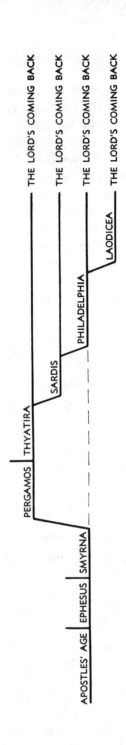

CHAPTER SEVEN

THE CHURCH IN PHILADELPHIA

Scripture Reading: Rev. 3:7-13; Matt. 23:8-11; John 20:17; 1 Cor. 12:13; Gal. 3:28

Here we have drawn a systematic chart. Perhaps it can help us to better understand. The first part represents the church in the apostles' age. Although Ephesus was a church which had already slackened, it is on the same straight line, since the Lord acknowledged that the church in Ephesus continued the apostolic church. Then came Smyrna, which also continued the line. Smyrna is really a suffering church. There is no praise nor rebuke for her. After Smyrna, however, something occurred when Pergamos appeared. She did not continue the orthodoxy of the apostles; she was united with the world and took a turn downward. She succeeded the church in Smyrna, but she did not continue in the orthodoxy of the apostles. Since Pergamos made such a turn, Thyatira followed in her steps. She took the same line as Pergamos, which was not the same as the apostles'. Sardis came out of Thyatira and she also made a turn, but her turn was one which headed back. Thyatira will continue until the Lord's coming, and Sardis will also continue until the Lord's coming.

Now it is our desire to introduce Philadelphia. Philadelphia is the church which returns to the orthodoxy of the apostles. Philadelphia also has a turn, a turn back to the position at the beginning of the Bible. The turn of recovery started with Sardis and was completed with Philadelphia. Now it is again on the same straight line as the age of the apostles. Philadelphia came out of Sardis. She is neither the Roman Catholic Church nor the Protestant churches, but continues the church at the age of the apostles. Later came Laodicea, which we will see when we come to her. Now we will spend some time to see what Philadelphia is, hoping that we may be clear regarding what she signifies.

Among the seven churches, five are rebuked and two are not. The two that are not rebuked are Smyrna and Philadelphia. The Lord approves only of these two. It is indeed remarkable that the words spoken by the Lord to Philadelphia are quite similar to those which were spoken to Smyrna. The problem of Smyrna was Judaism, while with Philadelphia there was also Judaism. To the church in Smyrna the Lord said, "That you may be tried" (Rev. 2:10), while to the church in Philadelphia the Lord said, "I also will keep you out of the hour of trial, which is about to come on the whole inhabited earth, to try them who dwell on the earth" (3:10). The Lord also spoke to the two churches regarding the crown. To Smyrna He said, "I will give you the crown of life" (2:10), while to Philadelphia He said, "Hold fast what you have that no one take your crown" (3:11). These two churches have these two points of similarity to show that they are on the same line, that is, on the line of the orthodoxy of the apostolic church. The church in Sardis was a recovery, but not a complete recovery; it was an incomplete recovery. But Philadelphia recovers to the point of meeting the Lord's desire. The church in Philadelphia not only receives no rebuke as Smyrna, but she is also praised. The straight line which we have drawn is the line of the chosen. We know that the Lord chose Philadelphia. Philadelphia continues the orthodoxy of the apostles. She recovers to Smyrna. Thus, the Lord's words to her are for us to keep and for us to obey. The turn of Pergamos and Thyatira was to such an extent that when Sardis came, she did not recover to completion even though she acted exceedingly great. Although she turned in the direction of recovery, she did not succeed in reaching the goal. Philadelphia is a complete recovery. Concerning this, I hope we may see clearly.

Philadelphia in Greek is composed of two words: The first means "love one another," and the second means "brother." Therefore, *Philadelphia* means "brotherly love." "Brotherly love" is the Lord's prophecy. Sacrifice is the special feature of Thyatira and is fulfilled in the Roman Catholic Church.

Recovery is the characteristic of Sardis and is fulfilled in the Protestant churches. Now the Lord tells us that there is a church which has been completely recovered and has been praised by Him. Those who read the Bible will raise the question, Who is this in actuality? Where can we find it in history? We cannot let this question pass easily.

I have already spoken of the behavior of the Nicolaitans and the teaching of the Nicolaitans in the church in Ephesus and the church in Pergamos. Moreover, I have indicated how they represent a class of priests. Among the Israelites the Levites could be the priests and the rest could not. But in the church all the children of God are priests. First Peter 2 and Revelation 5 tell us clearly that all who are bought with the blood are priests. Yet the Nicolaitans specifically created the office of the priest. The laity (common believers) must go to the world to take an occupation and perform secular affairs. The priests are above the laity and attend to the spiritual affairs. Now I will say something by way of repetition regarding the matter of the mediatorial class. The Jews have Judaism, and the Nicolaitans developed from a behavior to a teaching. We see the existence of a class of fathers. They attend to the spiritual affairs, while others take care of secular matters. The laying on of hands is their business; only they can bless. If we have to inquire concerning a certain matter, we cannot ask God ourselves; we must ask them to inquire of God for us. At the time of Sardis the condition improved. The system of the fathers was abolished, but the clergy system arose to take its place. In the Protestant churches there are the extremely strict state churches, and there are also the scattered private churches. However, whether it be a state or private church, the existence of the mediatorial class is always seen. The former has the clergy system while the latter has the pastoral system. Concerning the system of the priestly class, whether it is called fathers, clergy, or pastors, it is something which is rejected by the Lord. The Protestant churches are a change in form of the continuance of the Nicolaitan teaching found in Pergamos. Although in the Protestant churches no one is called a father, yet the clergy and pastors are exactly the same in principle.

Even if we change their name and call them workers, as long as they are standing in the same position, they have the same flavor.

I have already brought forth much Scripture as a basis for showing that we are all priests. But now there is an argument between God and men. Since God says that everyone in the church is qualified to be a priest, why do men say that spiritual authority is only in the hands of the mediatorial class such as the fathers? I repeat, as many as are redeemed with the precious blood are priests. Why does the Lord not rebuke Philadelphia, but rather praise her? Remember that the beginning of the mediatorial class was at Pergamos and the practice of the mediatorial class was in Rome. They have the popes who exercise dominion over them, they have the high officials exercising authority over them, and they have the Vatican (the church-palace) high officials, etc. But the Lord says, "You all are brothers." Hold fast to Matthew 23:8 and 20:26. The Bible does not have the system of pastors. The Lord said, "Do not call anyone on earth your father, for One is your Father....Neither be called instructors, because One is your Instructor" (23:9-10). But the Roman Catholic Church uses the term *father,* and the Protestant churches use the term *pastor.* In the nineteenth century there was a great revival which abolished the mediatorial class. A great recovery transpired after Sardis: The brothers loved one another, and the mediatorial class was abolished in the church. This is Philadelphia.

In 1825 in Dublin, the capital of Ireland, there were several believers whose hearts were moved by God to love all the children of the Lord, regardless of their denomination. This kind of love was not to be frustrated by the walls of denomination. They began to see that in the Scriptures God says there is but one Body of Christ, regardless of how many sects men may divide her into. They further read the Scriptures and saw that the system of one man administering the church and one man preaching was not scriptural. So they began to meet every Lord's Day to break bread and pray. In 1825—after more than a thousand years of the Roman Catholic Church and several hundred years of the Protestant churches—there was the first return to the simple, free, and spiritual worship in the Scriptures. At the beginning there were but two persons; later, there were four or five.

In the world's eyes these believers were lowly and unknown. But they had the Lord in their midst and the consolation of the Holy Spirit. They stood on the ground of two clear truths: First, the church is the Body of Christ and the Body is one, and second, there is no clergy system in the New Testament, that is, all the ministers of the Word set up by men are not scriptural. They believed that all true believers were the members of this one Body. They warmly welcomed all who came into their midst, regardless of their denomination. They did not have the consciousness of any sect. They believed that all true believers had the office of the priest and could freely enter into the Holy of Holies. They also believed the ascended Lord had given various gifts to the church for the perfecting of the saints, for the building up of the Body of Christ. Therefore, they were able to depart from the two sins of the clergy system—offering sacrifices and one man preaching the Word. These principles enabled them to welcome all who were in Christ as their brothers and to be open to all the ministers of the Word who were ordained by the Holy Spirit to serve.

During this time there was a clergyman in the Anglican Church by the name of John Nelson Darby who was very dissatisfied with the position of his own church, believing that it was not scriptural. He also met frequently with the brothers, although at that time he still wore the uniform of the Anglican clergy. He was a man of God, a man of great power, and a man willing to suffer. He was also a spiritual man who knew God and the Bible and judged the flesh. In 1827 he officially left the Anglican Church, put off the uniform of the clergy, and became a simple brother meeting together with the brothers. Originally what the brothers saw was rather limited, but when Darby joined, the light of heaven poured down like a torrent. In many aspects the work of Darby was similar to that of Wesley, but his attitude toward the Anglican Church was entirely different. In the previous century Wesley felt he could not leave the state church with peace; a century later Darby felt he could not continue in the

Anglican Church with peace. But as to zealousness, whole-heartedness, and faithfulness, they were alike in many aspects.

It was in that same year that J. G. Bellett also attended the meetings. He also was an exceedingly deep and spiritual man. This kind of meeting, which was simple yet scriptural, moved him greatly. Concerning the condition at that time, he had this to say:

A brother has just been telling me that it appeared to him from Scripture that believers, meeting together as disciples of Christ, were free to break bread together as their Lord had admonished them; and that, in as far as the practice of the apostles could be a guide, every Lord's day should be set apart for thus remembering the Lord's death and obeying his parting command.

At another time J. G. Bellett said:

Walking one day with a brother as we were passing down Lower Pembroke Street, he said to me: "This I doubt not is the mind of God concerning us—we should come together in all simplicity as disciples, not waiting on any pulpit or ministry, but trusting that the Lord would edify us together by ministering as He pleased and saw good from the midst of ourselves." At the moment he spoke these words, I was assured my soul had got the right idea, and that moment I remember as if it were but yesterday, and could point you out the place. It was the birthday of my mind, may I so speak, as a brother.

This was how the brothers groped gradually onward, received revelation gradually, and saw the light gradually. After one year in 1828, Darby published a little book called *The Nature and Unity of the Church of Christ*. This little book was the first among thousands of books published by the brothers. In this book Darby clearly declared that the brothers had no intention of setting up a new denomination or union of churches. He said:

In the first place, it is not a formal union of the outward professing bodies that is desirable; indeed it is surprising that reflecting Protestants should desire it: far from doing good, I conceive it would be impossible that such a body could be at all recognized as the church of God. It would be a counterpart to Romish unity; we should have the life of the church and the power of the word lost, and the unity of spiritual life utterly excluded... True unity is the unity of the Spirit, and it must be wrought by the operation of the Spirit...No meeting, which is not framed to embrace all the children of God in the full basis of the kingdom of the Son, can find the fulness of blessing, because it does not contemplate it—because its faith does not embrace it...Where two or three are gathered together in His name, His name is recorded there for blessing...

Further, unity is the glory of the church; but unity to secure and promote our own interests is not the unity of the church, but confederacy and denial of the nature and hope of the church. Unity, that is of the church, is the unity of the Spirit, and can only be in the things of the Spirit, and therefore can only be perfected in spiritual persons...

But what are the people of the Lord to do? Let them wait upon the Lord, and wait according to the teaching of His Spirit, and in conformity to the image, by the life of the Spirit, of His Son. Let them go their way forth by the footsteps of the flock, if they would know where the good Shepherd feeds His flock at noon.

In another place Darby said:

Because our table is the Lord's table, not our table, we receive all whom God receives, all poor sinners fleeing to the Lord for refuge, not resting in themselves, but only in Christ.

At that same time God worked simultaneously in British Guiana and Italy to raise up the same kind of meetings. In 1829 there were also meetings in Arabia. In 1830 in Great Britain's London, Plymouth, and Bristol, there were also meetings. Later, many places in the United States had meetings, and in the continent of Europe there were also many meetings. Not long afterwards, in almost every place in the entire world, all those who loved the Lord were meeting in this way. Although there was no outward union, yet all were raised up by the Lord.

One feature that marked the rising up of these brothers was that those who were titled and lorded gave up their titles and lordship, those with position gave up their position, those with degrees forsook their degrees, and everyone abandoned any worldly class or rank in the church and became simply the disciples of Christ and brothers one to another. Just as the word *father* is widely used in the Roman Catholic Church and *reverend* in the Protestant churches, so the word *brother* is commonly used in their midst. They were attracted by the Lord and thus met together; because of their love toward the Lord, they spontaneously loved one another.

Within the scores of years, from among these brothers God has given many gifts to His church. Besides J. N. Darby and J. G. Bellett, God granted special ministries to many of the brothers so that His church could be supplied. George Müller, who established an orphanage, recovered the matter of praying in faith. In his lifetime he had over 1,500,000 answers to prayer. C. H. Mackintosh, who wrote *Notes on the Pentateuch,* recovered the knowledge of types. D. L. Moody said that if all the books in the entire world were to be burnt, he would be satisfied to have just one copy of the Bible and a set of C. H. Mackintosh's *Notes on the Pentateuch.* James G. Deck gave us many good hymns. George Cutting recovered the assurance of salvation. His booklet "Safety, Certainty, and Enjoyment" sold thirty million copies by 1930. Other than the Bible it was the most widely sold writing. William Kelly wrote many expositions; he was described by C. H. Spurgeon as one whose mind was as big as the universe. F. W. Grant was the most learned of the Bible in the nineteenth and twentieth centuries. Robert Anderson was the man who best knew the book of Daniel in the recent age. Charles Stanley was the one who best brought people to salvation by preaching the righteousness of God. S. P. Tregelles was the famous New Testament philologist. The book on church history by Andrew

Miller was the most scriptural among the many church histories. R. C. Chapman was a man greatly used by the Lord. These were the brothers at that time. If we were to recount in detail others among the brothers, the number of all who were greatly used by the Lord would exceed at least a thousand.

Now we will see what these brothers gave us: They showed us how the blood of the Lord satisfies the righteousness of God; the assurance of salvation; how the weakest believer may be accepted in Christ, just as Christ was accepted; and how to believe in the Word of God as the foundation of salvation. Since church history began, there never was a period when the gospel was clearer than in their time. Not only so, it was also they who showed us that the church cannot gain the entire world, that the church has a heavenly calling, and that the church has no worldly hope. It was they who also opened up the prophecies for the first time, causing us to see that the return of the Lord is the hope of the church. It was they who opened the book of Revelation and the book of Daniel and showed us the kingdom, the tribulation, the rapture, and the bride. Without them, we would know a very small percentage of future things. It was also they who showed us what the law of sin is, what it is to be set free, what it is to be crucified with Christ, what it is to be raised with Christ, how to be identified with the Lord through faith, and how to be transformed daily by looking unto Him. It was they who showed us the sin of the denominations, the unity of the Body of Christ, and the unity of the Holy Spirit. It was they who showed us the difference between Judaism and the church. In the Roman Catholic Church and the Protestant churches, this difference could not be readily seen, but they made us see it anew. It was also they who showed us the sin of the mediatorial class, how all the children of God are priests, and how all can serve God. It was they who recovered for us the principle of meetings in 1 Corinthians 14, showing us that prophesying is not one man's business but the business of two or three, and that prophesying is not based upon ordination, but upon the gift of the Holy Spirit. If we were to enumerate one by one what they recovered, we may as well say that in today's pure Protestant churches there is not one truth that they did not recover or recover more.

It is no wonder that D. M. Panton said, "The movement of the brothers and its significance is far greater than the Reformation." W. H. Griffith Thomas said, "Among the children of God, it was they who were most able to rightly divide the word of truth." Henry Ironside said, "Whether among those who know the brothers or those who do not know the brothers, all those who know God have received help from the brothers directly or indirectly."

This movement was greater than the movement of the Reformation. Here I would like to say that the work of Philadelphia is greater than the work of the Reformation. Philadelphia gives us the things which the Reformation did not give us. We thank the Lord that the problem of the church is solved by the movement of the brothers. The position of the children of God has almost been recovered. Therefore, both in quantity and in quality you can see that it is greater than the Reformation. Yet we must note that the movement of the brothers is not quite as famous as the Reformation. The Reformation was brought about with sword and spear, while the movement of the brothers was brought about by preaching. For the cause of the Reformation, many lost their lives in the wars in Europe. Another reason the Reformation is famous was its relationship to politics. Many nations, through the Reformation, threw off the power of Rome politically. Anything that is not related to politics is not easily known by men. Furthermore, the brothers saw two things: One is what we call the organized world, that is, the psychological world; the other is what the brothers called the world of Christianity. They left not only the psychological world, but also the world of Christianity, which is represented by the Protestant churches. That is why they were not even advertised in the Protestant churches. They have come out not only from the world of sin, but also from the world of Christianity.

From their time, men knew that the church is the Body of Christ, that the children of God are one church, and that they should not be divided. Their emphasis was on the brothers and the real love for one another. The Lord Jesus says that a church will appear whose name is *Philadelphia.* Now let us look at Revelation: *"And to the messenger of the church in Philadelphia write"* (3:7). Philadelphia is brotherly love. What does the Lord praise Philadelphia for? He says it is brotherly love; the mediatorial position has been completely abolished. I will take this opportunity to say a few more words. In Christ there is neither male nor female. In Christ there are no sisters. We are brothers, not sisters. Now our sisters will ask, "Who are we?" We are all brothers. We are brothers because we all have the life of Christ. Today there are many men in the world, but they are not our brothers. A man is a brother not because he is man, but because he has the life of Christ in him. Since I also have the life of Christ in me, we are brothers. When the Lord resurrected and was about to ascend to heaven, He said, "I ascend to My Father and your Father" (John 20:17). In John 1 He is the only begotten Son of God; in John 20 He is God's firstborn Son. In chapter one God had Him as the only Son; in chapter twenty His life is imparted to men; thus, He is the firstborn Son and we all are brothers. Through death and resurrection God's only begotten Son became the firstborn Son. We can be brothers because we have received His life. Because we have all received the life of Christ, we are all brothers. A man is a brother because he receives the life of Christ; a woman is a brother because she receives the life of Christ. Both men and women all receive the same life; therefore, all are brothers. All the Epistles were written to brothers, not sisters. Individually speaking, there are sisters, but in Christ there are only brothers. Because of that life, we have become the children *(teknia)* of God. All the "sons and daughters" in the New Testament should be translated as "children." Besides 2 Corinthians 6:18, there is no mention of daughters. Do you see? In Christ everyone stands in the position of a brother. Once when I was in Shanghai, there was a brother who was a mason. I said to him, "Go and ask some brothers to come in." He replied, "Do you want me to ask the male brothers or the female brothers?" This was a man taught of God. We address sisters when we address individuals, but in Christ there is no distinction between male and female.

In the church there is also neither bond nor free. It is not that one receives more life because he is a master, or that one receives less life because he is a slave. In the past a certain brother told me that the meeting places were usually in poor condition, and that it would be best for us to prepare a place especially for preaching to the government officials. I replied, "What would you put on the signboard?" It would not be the church of Christ, but the church of the officials and gentry. When we come to the church, there are no officials or gentry. In the church all are brothers. When our eyes are opened by the Lord, we will see that being above others is a glory in the world, but that there is no such distinction in the church.

Paul says that in Christ there is neither Jew nor Greek, slave nor free, male nor female (Gal. 3:28). The church does not stand on distinction but on brotherly love.

In Revelation 3:7, as in the beginning of the other epistles, the Lord refers to Himself: *"These things says the Holy One, the true One, the One who has the key of David, the One who opens and no one will shut, and shuts and no one opens."* Holiness is His life; He Himself is holiness. He is the truth before God; He is God's reality, and God's reality is Christ. His hand holds the key. Here I would ask you to note one thing: When Sardis stood to witness for the Lord, there were the rulers of this world who helped her fight the battle. The fighting went on in the continent of Europe for scores of years and then in Great Britain for scores of years. But what about the movement of the brothers? There was no power at their back for support. What could they do? The Lord said that He holds the key of David, which means the authority. (The Bible calls David a king.) It is not a matter of force of arms, it is not a matter of advertising, but it is a matter of opening the door. There was a certain newspaper editor in Great Britain who said, "I never thought there were so many brothers, and I never knew these people could grow so fast." By traveling around the world, you will discover that in every place there are many brothers. Although some know the teachings in a deeper way and some shallowly, the position of the brothers is still the same. Seeing this, we should thank the Lord. The Lord says that He is the One who *"opens and no one will shut, and shuts and no one opens."* *"I know your works...because you have a little power"* (v. 8). When we reach this point, our thoughts spontaneously return to the time of Zerubbabel's return, of which a certain prophet said, "For who has despised the day of small things?" (Zech. 4:10). Do not despise the day of small things, that is, the day of building the temple. In the Scriptures there is a very great type of the church—the temple. When David reigned as king, the people of God were united. Later, they were divided into the kingdom of Judah and the kingdom of Israel. The children of God began to be divided, and at the same time idolatry and fornication commenced. As a result they were captured and taken to Babylon. Everyone acknowledges that the captivity in Babylon is a type of Thyatira—the Roman Catholic Church. Since the Bible makes Babylon a type of Rome, the church also has a Babylonian captivity. What did the people of God do when they returned from their captivity? They returned rather weakly, group by group, and built the temple. It seems that they were a type of the movement of the brothers. There were many elderly Jews who had seen the old temple. When they saw with their own eyes the laying of the foundation of the temple, they wept with a loud voice, for the temple was far inferior in glory compared to the temple in Solomon's time. Yet God spoke through the minor prophet, saying that they should not despise the day of small things, for it was the day of recovery. The Lord says similar words to Philadelphia: *"You have a little power."* When compared with the days of Pentecost, the testimony of the church in the world today is that this is the day of small things.

"You...have kept My word and have not denied My name" (Rev. 3:8). The Lord acknowledges them for two things: not denying the name of the Lord and not denying the word of the Lord. There has never been an age in church history in which there were men who knew the Word of God as much as the brothers. The light was like the downpour of a great torrential flood. When I was in Shanghai one night, I met a

certain brother who said he was a cook on a boat. I spoke
with him at length. I am afraid that very few missionaries
know the Word of God as well as He. Indeed, this is one of
their outstanding characteristics—they know the Word of
God. Even if you meet the simplest one among them, he will
be clearer than many missionaries.

The Lord also said, *"You...have not denied My name."*
Since 1825 the brothers said that they could only be called
Christians. If you ask them who they are, they will say, "I
am a Christian." But if you ask someone of the Methodist
Church, he will say, "I am a Methodist." If you meet one from
the Friends Church, he will say, "I belong to the Friends
Church." Someone from the Lutheran Church will reply, "I
am a Lutheran." Someone from the Baptist Church will say,
"I am a Baptist." Besides Christ, men still call themselves by
many other names. But the children of God have only one
name with which to call themselves. The Lord Jesus said,
"Ask in My name," and "Gathered into My name" (John 16:26;
Matt. 18:20). We can only have the Lord's name. Whitefield
said, "Let all other names be abandoned; let only the name
of Christ be exalted." These brothers rose up to do just that.
The Lord's prophecy says the same thing, that is, that they
honored the name of the Lord. The name of Christ is their
center. They hear this word in their midst quite often: "Is
the name of Christ not enough to separate us from the world?
Is it not sufficient simply to bear the name of the Lord?"

I met a certain believer once on a train who asked me
what kind of Christian I was. I replied that I was just a
Christian. He said, "There is no such Christian in the world.
Saying that you are a Christian means nothing; you have to
say what kind of Christian you are in order for it to be
meaningful." I replied, "I am simply a man who is a Christian.
Do you say that for a man to be a Christian means nothing?
What kind of Christian would you say is meaningful? As for
me, I can only be a Christian—nothing more." That day we
had a very good talk together.

I would like you to see one thing: The basic thought of
many people is that the name of the Lord is not enough.
Many think they need the name of a denomination; they

think they must have another name in addition to the name of the Lord. Brothers, do not think that our attitude is too determined. The Lord said, *"You...have not denied My name."* If my feeling is right, all other names are a shame to Him. This word "denied" is the same word used to describe Peter's denial of the Lord. What kind of a Christian am I? I am a Christian. I do not want to be called by another name. Many do not want to honor the name of Christ and are not willing just to be called a Christian. But thank God, the prophecy of Philadelphia was fulfilled in the brothers. They no longer have any other distinguishing name. They are brothers; they are not "The Brethren Church."

"Behold, I have put before you an opened door which no one can shut" (Rev. 3:8). The Lord speaks to the church in Philadelphia about the open door. Men often say that if you walk according to the Scriptures, the door will soon be shut; the most difficult hurdle to pass in submitting to the Lord is the shutting of the door. But here is indeed a promise: *"Behold, I have put before you an opened door which no one can shut."* As far as the brothers are concerned, this is a fact. In the whole world, whether in Bible exposition or gospel preaching, no group of people has had the opportunities they have had. Whether in Europe, America, or Africa, it has all been like this. There is no need of men's support, advertisement, propaganda, or contributions; they still have many opportunities to work, and the door for work is still open.

"Behold, I will make those of the synagogue of Satan, those who call themselves Jews and are not, but lie—behold, I will cause them to come and fall prostrate before your feet and to know that I have loved you" (v. 9). We have already seen at least four things which have caused Christianity to become Judaism: the mediatorial priests, the laws of letters, the material temple, and the earthly promises. What does the Lord say? *"I will cause them to come and fall prostrate before your feet."* Judaism is destroyed in the hands of the brothers. Everywhere in the whole world there is such a movement. Wherever they are, Judaism is defeated. Among those who really know God today, the principal strength of Judaism has become something of the past.

"Because you have kept the word of My endurance" (v. 10). This is connected with Revelation 1:9, which speaks of John being a "fellow partaker in the tribulation and kingdom and endurance in Jesus." "Endurance" is used as a noun. Today is the time of Christ's endurance. Today the Lord meets many who scorn Him, but He endures. His word today is the word of endurance. Here He has no reputation; He is a lowly person, still a Nazarene, still the son of a carpenter. When we follow the Lord, He says that we should keep the word of His endurance.

"I also will keep you out of the hour of trial, which is about to come on the whole inhabited earth, to try them who dwell on the earth" (3:10). We can use Chungking for an illustration: To say that I will keep you from the bombing means that you will still be in Chungking, but that you will be kept from the bombing. If I say I will keep you from the hour, that means that before that hour you will have just left for Ch'eng-tu. When the whole world is being tried (we all know that this refers to the great tribulation), we will not meet the tribulation. Before that hour arrives, we will have been raptured already. In the whole Bible there are only two passages which speak of the promise of rapture: Luke 21:36 and Revelation 3:10. Today we must follow the Lord, not live loosely, learn to walk in the way of Philadelphia, and ask the Lord to deliver us from all the trials to come.

"I come quickly; hold fast what you have that no one take your crown" (3:11). The Lord says, "I come quickly"; therefore, this church is to continue until the Lord comes back. Thyatira is not gone, Sardis is not gone, and Philadelphia is not gone. *"Hold fast what you have,"* which is *"My word"* and *"My name."* We should not forget the word of the Lord, and we should not put the Lord's name to shame. *"That no one take your crown."* All of Philadelphia have the crown already. In the other churches it is a problem of gaining the crown; here it is a problem of losing it. The Lord says that they already have the crown. In the whole Bible only one person knew he had the crown—Paul (2 Tim. 4:8). So also among the churches, only Philadelphia knows that she has the crown. Do not let any man take your crown; do not come out from Philadelphia

and leave your position. Here it says to hold fast what you have that no man take it.

This tells us clearly that Philadelphia also has her own particular danger; otherwise, the Lord would not have given her such a warning. Moreover, this danger is quite real, which is why the Lord commands her in such a serious manner. What is her danger? Her danger lies in losing what she already has. So the Lord asks her to hold fast what she has. Her danger is not in failing to progress; rather, it is in retrogression. Those in Philadelphia are pleasing to the Lord because they love one another and are faithful to the Lord's word and the Lord's name. Their danger lies in losing this love and faithfulness. How dreadful! But in fact this is what has actually happened. After twenty years the brothers were divided. They were divided into two divisions: "Exclusive" and "Open," and within the two divisions there are many sects. Therefore, in Philadelphia there is also the call to the overcomers.

What is the reason for this problem? We must be very careful and humble or else we will become involved in the same failure. I think any kind of division is due to the lack of love for one another; when love does not exist or is lacking, people pay attention to laws, stress procedures, and split hairs to find faults. Once love is in distress, people will also be proud of themselves and envious of others, which produces controversy and strife. The Holy Spirit is the strength of oneness, while the flesh is the strength of division. Unless the flesh is dealt with, division will occur sooner or later.

Furthermore, I believe the lack at that time was that the brothers *did not see the "local" ground and boundary of the church.* They clearly saw the sins of the church on the negative side, but on the positive side, *they did not adequately see how the church should love one another and be of one accord on the ground and boundary of locality.* The Roman Catholic Church pays attention to the oneness of a united church on this earth, while the Brethren paid attention to an idealistic oneness of a spiritual church in heaven. They did not see or did not see clearly enough that the love for one another in the epistles is the love for one another in the church in one locality; the oneness is the oneness of the church in one locality; the joining together is the joining together of the church in one locality; the edification is the edification of the church in a locality; and even the excommunication is the excommunication of the church in one locality. In any case, only these two kinds of people talk about the oneness of the church: The Roman Catholic Church speaks of the unity of all the churches on this earth, while the Brethren speak of the spiritual oneness in heaven. As a result, the former is but a oneness in outward appearance, while the latter is an idealistic oneness that is, in fact, divisive. *Both have not noticed the oneness of each and every local church in each and every locality as recorded in the Bible.*

Since *the Brethren did not pay enough attention to the fact that the church has the locality as her boundary,* the "Exclusive Brethren" demanded unified action throughout in every place, resulting in breaking the boundary of locality and falling into the error of the united church; while the "Open Brethren" demanded independent administration of every meeting, the result of which is that there are many places that have many churches in one locality, thus falling into the error of the Congregational Church, which makes each congregation an independent unit. *The "Exclusive Brethren" exceed the boundary of locality, while the "Open Brethren" are smaller than the boundary of locality. They forget that in the Bible there is one and only one church in every locality.* The words spoken in the Bible to the church are spoken to this kind of church. Strangely enough, today's inclination is to change the words spoken in the Bible to the local church to words spoken to the spiritual church. Moreover, when some brothers set up the church, they set up a church that is smaller than the locality—the "house" church is a case in point. But in the Bible there is no "United Church" of the churches everywhere; neither are there churches of the congregations and meetings in one locality as independent churches. One church for several localities or several churches in one locality—both are not ordained of God. God's Word clearly reveals that *one locality can have only one church, and there can only be one church in one locality.* To have one church in several localities demands a unity which the Bible does not demand; to have several churches in one locality divides the oneness which the Bible demands. The difficulty of the Brethren in those days was that *they were not clear enough regarding the teaching in the Bible on locality.* The result is that since those who have the "United Church" type of unity are united with brothers in other places, they are not afraid to be divided from brothers in the same locality. Similarly, those who take the meeting as a unit and who have no problem with the brothers in the same meeting are not afraid to be divided with the brothers who are in other meetings in the same locality. Because *they have not realized the importance of the teachings in the Bible concerning the locality,* divisions have resulted in both cases. The Lord does not demand the impractical unity of all places. The Lord also does not permit taking one meeting as the boundary of unity—that is too free; it is licentious, having no restriction or lesson. With just one word of disagreement, another meeting is formed immediately with three to five as a group, and this is counted as oneness. *There can only be one kind of oneness in a locality.* What a restriction to those with fleshly license!

The movement of the brothers is still in progress, *and the light of "locality" is clearer and clearer.* To what extent the Lord will work we do not know. We can only wait for history; then we will be clear. If our consecration to the Lord is absolute and we ourselves are humble, it may be that we will receive mercy to be kept from error.

"He who overcomes, him I will make a pillar in the temple of My God, and he shall by no means go out anymore, and I will write upon him the name of My God and the name of the city of My God, the New Jerusalem, which descends out of heaven from My God, and My new name" (Rev. 3:12). During the time of Philadelphia there have been many cases of excommunicating the brothers. But here they can no longer be excommunicated; they will be a pillar in the temple of God. If the pillar is removed, the temple cannot stand. Philadelphia makes the temple of God stand. There are three names written on the overcomer—the name of God, the name

of the New Jerusalem, and the Lord's new name. God's eternal plan is accomplished. The people in Philadelphia return to the Lord and satisfy Him.

"He who has an ear, let him hear what the Spirit says to the churches" (v. 13). Please remember, God has not kept His heart's desire in secret; God has put the way very clearly before us.

CHAPTER EIGHT

THE CHURCH IN LAODICEA

Scripture Reading: Rev. 3:14-22

Now we will speak of the last church. We have seen the Roman Catholic Church, the Protestant churches, and the movement of the brothers. Among these, God has chosen the movement of the brothers. Thyatira entirely failed. Although Sardis was better than Thyatira, the Lord still rebuked them. Only Philadelphia did not receive a word of rebuke. The Lord's promise is in Philadelphia. (But Philadelphia also has a calling for overcomers.) If it were up to us, we would have stopped with Philadelphia and written nothing more. However, in these churches the Lord prophesies concerning the condition of the church; therefore, it is necessary to take a step further to Laodicea, with which everyone is most familiar. If you asked which church Laodicea refers to, many could not answer. Many of God's children are not clear concerning Laodicea. Some think of learning lessons from her as individuals; some consider her as referring to the general, desolate condition of the church. But the Lord is speaking prophecy here.

Laodicea, just like the other churches, has special meaning in her name. It is composed of two words: *laos,* meaning "laymen" (laity or common people), and *dicea,* which may be translated as "customs" or "opinions." So Laodicea means the customs of the laymen or the opinions of the common people. Here we see very clearly the meaning—the church has already failed. The church has turned to the pattern of taking the opinions and customs of the laymen. In Philadelphia we see brothers and love for one another. But here we see laymen, opinions, and customs.

Please remember one thing: If the children of God do not stand in the position of Philadelphia, they will fall and fail. However, they cannot return to Sardis. Once a person has seen the truth of the brothers, he can no longer go back to the Protestant churches, even if he wants to. Since he is not able to stand firmly in Philadelphia, he retrogresses from Philadelphia to become, as here, Laodicea. That which came out from the Roman Catholic Church is called the Protestant church; that which came out from the Protestant churches is called the brothers; and that which goes forth from Philadelphia is called Laodicea. Sardis comes out of Thyatira, and Philadelphia comes out of Sardis; likewise, Laodicea goes out of Philadelphia. God's children today have a misunderstanding; that is, whenever they see a certain denominational church, the condition of which is wrong, they say that that is Laodicea. That is wrong. A wrong denominational church is Sardis, not Laodicea. The different denominations are the Protestant churches. The denominations are not qualified to become Laodicea. Only failing Philadelphia can become Laodicea. The condition of Laodicea is not the condition of Sardis. Only that which has tasted the goodness of Philadelphia and is now fallen is Laodicea. That which actually does not have much is Sardis. That which does not keep the spiritual riches in the Holy Spirit becomes Laodicea.

What kind of a fall then is this? Beginning with Ephesus we see abnormality in the midst of normality. In Pergamos we see the teaching of Balaam. In Thyatira we see Jezebel; the mediatorial class has its root there. Sardis gives us an open Bible, but Sardis herself creates another mediatorial class. In Philadelphia we see only brothers; the class that conquers the laity no longer exists. Everyone comes back to the word of the Lord to obey the Lord's word and to obey what the Holy Spirit has spoken through the word of the Lord. But one day, by not standing in the position of brothers who receive the discipline of the Holy Spirit and by falling from the position of brothers to that of laymen, Laodicea appears. In Sardis the authority lies in the hands of the pastoral system. In Philadelphia the authority lies in the hands of the Holy Spirit; the Holy Spirit exercises authority through the word and the name, and all are brothers loving one another. Now in Laodicea it is neither the Holy Spirit exercising the authority nor the pastoral system, but the laymen. What do we mean by laymen exercising authority? We mean exercising the authority of the majority. The opinion of the majority is the accepted opinion; as long as the majority is in favor, it is all right. This is Laodicea. In other words it is not the fathers who rule, nor the pastors, nor the Holy Spirit, but the opinion of the majority that counts. Here it is not brothers, but men. Laodicea does not stand in the position of brothers; rather, it is men who are according to the will of the flesh. Everyone raises the hand, and that is all. We must know the will of God and look at Philadelphia according to the will of God. Whenever there is no brotherly love but only the opinions of men according to the flesh, you meet Laodicea.

Here the Lord speaks of Himself as *"the Amen, the faithful and true Witness, the beginning of the creation of God"* (Rev. 3:14). The Lord is Amen. Amen means all right; it means "so let it be." Thus, He will fulfill everything, and nothing will be in vain. The Lord Jesus testified of the work of God on the earth. Among the many beings and things created by God, the Lord is the Head.

"I know your works, that you are neither cold nor hot; I wish that you were cold or hot. So, because you are lukewarm and neither hot nor cold, I am about to spew you out of My mouth" (vv. 15-16). Sardis is living in name, but dead in reality; Laodicea is neither hot nor cold. To Ephesus the Lord said, "I am coming to you and will remove your lampstand out of its place" (2:5). To Laodicea He said, "I am about to spew you out of My mouth." The Lord will not use them again; they are no longer the amen. The problem is that they are neither cold nor hot. They are filled with knowledge, yet lacking in power. When they were hot, they were Philadelphia; but now they are colder than before. Once Philadelphia falls, she becomes Laodicea. Only the people of Philadelphia can fall to such an extent.

"Because you say, I am wealthy and have become rich and have need of nothing" (3:17). I have mentioned already that

the movement of the brothers is far more significant than the Reformation. The Reformation was but a reformation in quantity, while the movement of the brothers was a reformation in quality, recovering the original substance of the church. This power is really great. But because these brothers were stronger than others in conduct and in truth to the point that even a cook among them knew more than a missionary in the Protestant churches, they became proud. "You are all incompetent; only we are competent," was their attitude. No one was competent in the Protestant churches. The famous Scofield went to the brothers to be taught. Gypsy Smith, so widely known, went into their midst to obtain profit, taking their doctrines to preach. All workers, students, preachers, and believers received help and light from them. We do not know how many more received help from their books. Many must acknowledge in their hearts that in the entire world, no one can teach the Bible as well as the brothers. As a result some of them became proud. "Our students are the teachers of others," they say. Although they are greatly opposed, some are self-declared heroes. The most evident result is that some became self-satisfied. Some brothers do have brotherly love and seek the good of others, while others have nothing but knowledge. Therefore, it was inevitable that they become self-exalted and conceited. The Lord shows us that a proud Philadelphia is Laodicea, and Laodicea is a fallen Philadelphia. Consequently, in many places the meetings in their midst have trouble with their behavior and teaching. The special feature of Laodicea is spiritual pride. As far as the historical side is concerned, the Lord has fulfilled this for us.

We can meet Philadelphia today, and we can also meet Laodicea. Both are quite alike in their position as the church. The difference is that Philadelphia has love while Laodicea has pride. There is no difference in outward appearance; the only difference is that Laodicea is a proud Philadelphia. I do not wish to relate many things concerning them. I will just give you some illustrations. A brother among them once said, "Is there anything spiritual that cannot be found among us?" A certain brother, after seeing a new magazine, said, "What new thing can it give us? Is there anything that we do not have?" He returned the magazine without reading it any further. Another brother said, "Since the Lord has given us the greatest light, we should be satisfied; if we read what others have written it is a waste of time." Another said, "What do others have that we do not have?" And still another said, "What others have, we have, but what we have, others may not have." When we hear this kind of talk, we should immediately recall what the Lord says regarding those who say, "I am rich." Oh, how careful we must be that we may not become Laodicea!

On an island in the Atlantic Ocean, there was a hurricane which destroyed many houses, including the homes and meeting halls of the brothers. Within a few hours brothers from all over the world sent them more than two hundred thousand pounds sterling, the relief reaching them more swiftly than that of the government. In their midst there is really brotherly love, but there are also those who have become proud. The Protestant churches are not qualified to become Laodicea. Sardis herself acknowledges that she has nothing. I have been working for more than twenty years, yet I have never met a missionary or pastor in the denominations who claims that they have the spiritual things. They always say they are inadequate. The failing and weak Protestant churches are Sardis, not Laodicea. Only Laodicea has the special feature of spiritual pride. The Protestant churches have many sins, but spiritual pride is not their outstanding sin. Only the fallen brothers would say, "I am wealthy and have become rich and have need of nothing." Only fallen Philadelphia can become Laodicea. As to wealth of spirituality, Sardis knows quite well that she has nothing. They often say, "We are not zealous enough; our zealous members have run away." Richness is the condition of Philadelphia, while boasting of their richness is the distinguishing mark of Laodicea. Only Laodicea can boast. A person who departs from the position of Philadelphia cannot go back to Sardis. Asking a brother to go back to Sardis is an impossibility; he can only go on to be Laodicea. Laodicea also does not continue the line of the orthodoxy of the apostles. She goes beyond the line of the apostles. They are those who have vain knowledge; they have no life and are self-satisfied, self-exalted, and conceited. *"And do not know that you are wretched and miserable and poor and blind and naked"* (v. 17). What they say is really quite true: I am wealthy and have become rich and have need of nothing! Indeed, they are marvelous before God. They have reason to boast. We acknowledge that there are many things in their midst of which they may boast. But it is better to leave this to the feeling of others and not to feel it ourselves; let others know about it, not ourselves. It would indeed be good if others say so; but if we say so, it is not good. Spiritual things must not be boasted of. If one boasts of his riches concerning worldly things, the money will not fly away nor will the amount decrease; but spiritual things vanish away when you boast of them. When a person says he is strong, then that strength is gone. The face of Moses shone, yet he himself was not aware of it. Whoever knows that his face is shining will lose the shining of his face. If you do not know you are growing, you are blessed. There are many who are so clear about their own condition, but on the contrary they have nothing. If you have spiritual authority, that is all right, but if you know you have spiritual authority, that is not all right. The Laodiceans are too clear in the estimate of themselves; they have too much. In God's eyes they are blind, poor, and naked. That is why we must learn the lesson. Laodicea is too clear regarding her richness. We hope that we will grow, yet we do not want to know it ourselves.

The Lord said, *"You are wretched."* The word "wretched" here is the same as the word "wretched" used by Paul in Romans 7:24. The Lord is saying that they are just like Paul in Romans 7: On the spiritual side they are wretched, they are embarrassed, they are not like this and not like that, and in the Lord's eyes they are miserable. Following this, the Lord points out three reasons why they are wretched and miserable: They are poor, they are blind, and they are naked.

Concerning poverty, the Lord said, *"I counsel you to buy from Me gold refined by fire that you may be rich"* (Rev. 3:18). Although they are rich in doctrines, the Lord sees them as still being poor. They must have living faith; otherwise, God's

Word is useless to them. Their failure, their weakness, is due to the fact that their faith is gone. Peter says that gold proved by fire is faith on trial (1 Pet. 1:7). In days when the word given forth is poor, you must pray. When the word increases, you must have faith that mingles with the words you have heard. You must pass through all manner of trials so that the words which you have heard will be useful in a practical way. Thus, you must buy gold tried in the fire. You must learn to trust even while in tribulation; then you will really be rich.

Moreover, the Lord says, *"And white garments that you may be clothed and that the shame of your nakedness may not be manifested"* (Rev. 3:18). We have already mentioned that the "white garment" refers to behavior. The "white garment" here is the same as the white garment spoken of in several other places in Revelation. God's purpose is that they should have no contamination, just as the garment is white. God wants them to walk continuously before Him. It is impossible to be naked before God. In the Old Testament no man could approach God without being clothed. When the priests went to the altar, their nakedness was not to be discovered. Second Corinthians 5:3 says, "If indeed, being clothed, we will not be found naked." But here it is not a matter of being clothed or unclothed, but a matter of whether or not the garment is white. The Lord Jesus says, "And whoever gives to one of these little ones only a cup of cold water to drink in the name of a disciple, truly I say to you, he shall by no means lose his reward" (Matt. 10:42). This is the white garment. We may treat others with a feast, yet it may not be "white." If we do it just for the sake of maintaining the glory of our group, that cannot be counted; if it springs from a motive that is even meaner than this, there is even a lesser reason for it to be counted. It is not clean enough. The Lord desires that we have a clean purpose and a clean motive to work for Him. There are many activities and many motives in which we sense many impurities once we touch them; they are not white. *"That the shame of your nakedness may not be manifested."* When we walk before God, we should not be shameful.

The Lord also speaks of buying *"eyesalve to anoint your eyes that you may see"* (Rev. 3:18). Buy eyesalve to anoint your eyes—this is the revelation of the Holy Spirit. You must have the revelation of the Holy Spirit; then you can be counted as seeing. On the contrary, knowing too much doctrine may result in the decrease of the revelation of the Holy Spirit. Doctrine is the transmission of thought from one to another; yet the spiritual eyes have not seen. Many people are walking in the light of others. Many elderly brothers speak in this way, so you speak in this way. Today you say, "So-and-so told me"; if there were no "So-and-so" to tell you, you would not know what to do. You receive doctrine from man's teaching, not from the Lord Jesus. The Lord Jesus says that this will not work; you must have the revelation of the Holy Spirit. I cannot write a letter to a friend asking him to listen to the gospel for me so that I can be saved. Likewise, anything received from the hands of man is finished when it comes to us; it has nothing to do with God. According to the Bible, this is blindness. Without touching the Holy Spirit, you cannot deal with spiritual things. It is not a matter of how much you have heard. Many times it is merely an increase in doctrine, an increase in knowledge, yet without seeing anything before God. So you must learn one thing before God—you have to buy eyesalve. Only seeing by myself is really seeing. Seeing is the basis of what has already been gained and is the basis of seeing again.

"As many as I love I rebuke and discipline; be zealous therefore and repent" (v. 19). The words spoken previously are rebukes. But the Lord shows us that He rebukes and chastens in this manner because He loves. Therefore, be zealous. What should we do? Repent. First, we must repent. Repentance is not just an individual matter; the church also must repent.

"Behold, I stand at the door and knock; if anyone hears My voice and opens the door, then I will come in to him and dine with him and he with Me" (v. 20). There is quite a lot in this statement. What kind of door is this door? Many use this verse to preach the gospel. It is all right to borrow this verse for the preaching of the gospel; it is all right to lend this verse to the sinners; but it must not be borrowed too

long without returning it. This verse is a verse for the children of God. It does not refer to the Lord knocking at the heart of a sinner; this door is the door of the church. Because the door here is singular, the Lord is referring to the church. It is indeed strange that the Lord is the Head of the church, or shall we say the origin of the church, yet He is standing outside the door of the church! *"Behold, I stand at the door"!* This is really a terrible condition. If the Lord is outside the door of the church, what kind of church is this?

The Lord says, "Behold"! The Lord says this to the whole church. The door is the door of the church. "If anyone hears My voice and opens the door..." These two words—"if anyone"—show that the opening of the door is an individual matter. In the Bible there are two lines in regard to the truth. One line is the line of the Holy Spirit, and the other line is the line of Christ; one is subjective, and the other is objective; one concerns experience, and the other concerns the faith. If someone pays too much attention to the objective truth, then he can be seen mounting the clouds and riding the mists, which is impractical. If he constantly stands on the subjective side, excessively stressing the inner working of the Holy Spirit, then he will look continuously inward and become dissatisfied. Everyone who is seeking the Lord must be balanced by both truths. One shows me that I am perfect in Christ, and the other shows me that the inner working of the Holy Spirit causes me to become perfect. The greatest failure of the Brethren was their excessive stress on the objective truth and neglect of the subjective truth. Philadelphia failed and became Laodicea. Her failure was due to too much objective truth. This does not mean that there was nothing at all of the inner working of the Holy Spirit, but generally speaking, there was too much of the objective aspect with too little of the subjective. If you open the door, "I will come in." This means that the objective becomes the subjective; that is, He will change what you have of the objective into the subjective. In John 15:4 the Lord speaks of both aspects: "Abide in Me and I in you." In Revelation 3:20 the Lord says, "I will come in to him and dine with him and he with Me." If you open the door, He will dine with you. This is fellowship and this also is joy. Then you will have an intimate fellowship with the Lord as well as the joy that springs from such fellowship.

"*He who overcomes, to him I will give to sit with Me on My throne, as I also overcame and sat with My Father on His throne*" (v. 21). Among the promises given to the overcomers in the seven churches, many say this is the best. Although some like the other promises to the overcomers, many have told me that the Lord's promise to Laodicea excels them all. In the previous promises to the overcomers the Lord did not say anything concerning Himself. But here the Lord says that if you overcome, you will dine with Me. Since you have passed through all kinds of overcoming, you can sit with My Father on the throne. You must overcome so that you can sit with the Lord on His throne. The overcomer here has an exceedingly high promise because the church age is ending. The overcomer is waiting for the coming of the Lord Jesus. Therefore, the throne is here.

CHAPTER NINE

CONCLUSION

In the Old Testament there are very clear prophecies concerning Judah. (Israel had no prophecy. Israel rebelled against God during the time of Jeroboam, and it was the nation which perished first. Evidently, God was not pleased with Israel and rejected her. So Israel had no prophecy.) Judah's prophecy continued through to the Lord Jesus— we can see this from the genealogy in Matthew 1. In the Old Testament there were many prophets whose work had no other purpose than to show us how things will be in the future. For example, Daniel prophesied concerning the condition of the nations. After Judah perished, Gentile nations would be raised up one by one in the following 2,500 years until the coming again of the Lord Jesus. Hence, well-known prophecies, such as those in Daniel 2, 7, 9, and 11, are very detailed concerning the Gentiles. In addition to the prophecies concerning Judah and the Gentiles, there is still the church of God in God's plan. Where is the prophecy concerning the church? When we read the first seven Epistles by Paul, there are no prophecies. It seems as if there are some in Matthew 13, but they are not detailed enough and not sufficiently clear in reference to the church, because they refer to the outward appearance of the kingdom of the heavens. Therefore, we may say that only Revelation 2 and 3, the latter seven epistles, show us the prophecy of the church. Thus far, we have briefly studied through each one and have seen that each has been fulfilled. We have already seen the prophecies which the Lord has shown us and the fulfillment given by history. We thank God that the prophecies have already been fulfilled; it is therefore much easier for us to read the seven epistles according to their fulfillment.

Through these seven epistles the Lord desires to provide us with a guide on how to be overcomers. The Lord is especially telling us how we should behave in order to overcome, and so, through the fulfillment of these epistles, He shows us the way to be an overcomer on this earth. Therefore, this is related to the way in which each one of us walks.

As we look at these seven epistles together, we see that each epistle is divided into four sections. From the first epistle to the last they are all alike. First there is the name of the Lord Himself, then the condition of the church, then the reward to the overcomer, and finally the calling to those who have ears. In each epistle the Lord shows us who He is, what the condition of the church is, what He will give to the overcomer, and then He appeals to those who have an ear that they may hear. There is a calling to the overcomers in every church; each has its own special feature, and the Lord's rewards to the overcomers are also different.

So we should learn that regardless of the condition the church, whenever any church has a problem, if we are faithful before the Lord, we will discover what we must do. The Lord shows us the way to deal with the problem. The Lord says He is the way, He is the reality, and He is the life (John 14:6). So no matter in which epistle and under what circumstances we are, the Lord does not want us to pay attention to the situation, however bad it may be; rather, He wants us to see who He is. Revelation recovers the seeing. Concerning the knowledge of the Lord, we see it by revelation just once. Once we see it, all failures pass away. We must see before God that the difficulty of the church is quite urgent. In this situation we cry for help, but the Lord says that only those who know Him have help. In each epistle the Lord makes one statement about who He is. Will such a Lord as He be able to deal with this situation?

As it is with the church, so it is with ourselves. In difficult circumstances, we must know the Lord who is contrary to our difficulty. Other problems are secondary. The solution to all problems depends on how much we know the Lord. Some are able to bear much, but some can bear only little. The strength to bear, whether much or little, depends on how much we know the Lord. Thus, at the beginning of each of the seven epistles, attention is given to who the Lord is. If a man does not know the Lord, he will not be able to know the church. Many are quite satisfied with the condition of the church today because they do not see. They have not seen who is sitting upon the throne, and they have not seen the different aspects of the glory of the Lord and His virtues. If we know the Lord, we will discover man's sin and the church's sin. The solution to the whole problem depends on how much we know the Lord. Those who only know a little of God have little revelation of God and are more tolerant with presumptuous things. But for each one who stands before the Lord, the Lord removes the toleration for that which is not according to His will. Once we receive revelation before the Lord, He removes everything that is not according to His will. Then we know that if we want to be holy, we will have the Lord; if we do not want to be holy, we will lose the fellowship of the Lord.

Regarding what we have seen concerning the things of the seven epistles, we must understand that we are arguing concerning the problem of the system. Please remember, all of the things in these seven epistles are related to the Lord. If we know the Lord, we will condemn God's people who walk according to their own wishes; if we do not know the Lord sufficiently, we will tolerate their walk according to their own desire. Many times we can tolerate the condition of Christians because we are not faithful enough to Christ. Our lack of faithfulness to the Lord is due to the fact that we still do not have revelation to know the Lord who condemns this as sin. Oh, there are even times when we must choose between the Lord and His people as to whom we must serve.

We already know that the number seven is divided into three and four. After Ephesus, there is Smyrna, and after Smyrna there is Pergamos. These three are of one group, because they have all passed away. The latter four are also of one group. Thyatira, Sardis, Philadelphia, and Laodicea are different from the first three. When Sardis is on this earth, Thyatira is on the earth; when Philadelphia is on this earth, Sardis is on the earth; and when Laodicea is on this earth, Philadelphia is also on the earth. In other words, the last four churches continue their days on the earth together. They do not begin at the same time, but they end at the same time.

The four churches before us today are very meaningful. When the Protestant churches appeared, the Roman Catholic Church had been present for more than a thousand years. When Philadelphia appeared, the Protestant churches had been present for more than three hundred years. When Laodicea appeared, Philadelphia had been present for several scores of years. We who are born in this age today are confronted with something very special: There are four different kinds of churches from which we may choose. If we were born before the fourteenth and fifteenth centuries, we would have no other way but to be in the Roman Catholic Church. If we were born in the eighteenth century, we could choose to belong to either the Roman Catholic Church or the Protestant churches. In the following century, in 1825, Philadelphia appeared and the brothers rose up; so we would have had three to choose from. Then after 1840, Laodicea appeared. Today there are four different kinds of churches. In all four there are people who are saved—some are better, and some are worse. God put us in a time where there are four ways from which we can choose.

But the Lord also shows us His desire. His desire is not the Roman Catholic Church; this question is past. There is not the least necessity of praying whether or not I should be a disciple of the pope. Although this prophecy is placed in Revelation 2, the need to decide whether or not to choose it no longer exists. All those who study the Bible know that the problem of choosing the Roman Catholic Church is over. There is a difficulty in the fact that many brothers do not know that the problem of choosing the Protestant churches is also over. Does the Lord want us to be in Sardis? Strangely enough, many are rather satisfied to be in Sardis. But if we read the Word of God, the Lord will show us that He is not satisfied with Sardis. The Lord's desire is Philadelphia. Of the seven epistles which we have seen, only Philadelphia is praised by the Lord. In the other epistles the Lord always gives some word of rebuke. Smyrna is better and has no rebuke, but neither does she have any praise. Philadelphia, however, is different. From beginning to end the Lord only praises her. Then you may ask whether we should join the movement of the brothers (as if this movement can be "joined"). Many people in the movement of the brothers have become Laodicea already. Then what should we do? Laodicea is also rejected by the Lord. If we are not careful, instead of catching up with Philadelphia, we will get into Laodicea.

There is a great problem today to which God's children must pay attention. Since 1921 in China, the gospel has become clearer and clearer, those who were saved have increased more and more, and God has directed our attention increasingly to the truth of the church. We began to see that the church is entirely of God, only those who are saved can be in it, and only the words which God has ordained in the Bible are to be kept by the church. During that time none of us ever heard of the movement of the brothers. Not until 1927 did we begin to hear of this kind of work abroad. Through literature which we continually received, we knew there was a very great movement going on, filling all the countries in the world. The Reformation was just such a great movement. But on the other hand, we felt that many among them had fallen into the position of Laodicea. At that time we had a question: What does the Bible say? Should the children of God join a movement? The unity of Christians should be in Christ, not in a movement. So we spent more time to study the Bible. We became increasingly clear that *that which is bigger than the locality is not the church, and that which is smaller than the locality is also not the church.*

In this age God shows us four different churches. We may put it in this way: There are the Roman Catholic Church, the Protestant churches, the brothers who love one another, and the Brethren Assemblies. The fourth one, the Brethren Assemblies, has fallen into the position of Laodicea. As far as this group is concerned, it has become a sect. I asked a certain brother, "Do you think I look like a brother?" He said, "Yes, you do, but in 'your' midst there still..." Immediately I replied, "Then what are 'you'? Is it not enough for me to be a brother? All those who are redeemed by the blood are included in 'us.'" If at any time there is a brother saved in Chungking, yet the church in Chungking says he is not a brother, then the church in Chungking has become a sect. A sect requires something more of a man who is a brother before they will call him a brother. Although they may not say that they are the Brethren Assembly, yet there is an invisible boundary placed there.

What kind of people are today's Philadelphia? The church in every place may be Philadelphia, and it also may not be. Actually, there is no way for me to say which one is and which one is not. Perhaps the church in Chungking is Philadelphia and the church in K'un-ming is not. Perhaps Cheng-tu's church is Philadelphia and Lan-chou's is not. Today it has become a problem of locality, just as the seven epistles are for localities. We must reject the Roman Catholic Church, and we must leave the Protestant churches. On the negative side, we can eliminate these two; but on the positive side, are we Philadelphia or still Laodicea? It is easy to withdraw from the Roman Catholic Church, and it is also easy to withdraw from the Protestant churches; all we need to do is write a letter and walk out the front door. But whether or not we are Philadelphia remains a question. This depends on whether or not we have walked out the back door. Philadelphia may not fall back to Sardis, but she may fall into Laodicea. The Lord's criticism of Laodicea is much stronger than His criticism of Sardis. The Lord wants us to learn to exalt His name, for where two or three are gathered together in the Lord's name, there He is in their midst. But we should never exalt ourselves. Whoever claims to be Philadelphia no longer appears as Philadelphia.

Today if you have left the denominations and have seen the church, then only the Word of God can be the standard. Consider a brother who is born again. Can you say that he is not a brother? He is a brother if he knows the truth clearly, and he is still a brother if he does not know the truth clearly. If he stays at home he is my brother, and if he falls into the ditch by the street he is still my brother. If there is a problem, I can only blame my Father for begetting him.

The special characteristic of Philadelphia is brotherly love—today this way is the only way for us to walk. But we should never have this kind of attitude: I love the brothers who are clear and the brothers who are lovable, but those who are not lovable I will not love. Whether he is clear or not, that is his business. We should never say, "You are a rebellious one." What we see this year, we did not see last year. Perhaps next year he will also see what we have seen this year. While he reads the Bible, the Lord will also show him the light. God's heart is great; so ours must also be great. We must learn to have a heart that is large enough to include all of God's children. Whenever we say "we" and yet do not include all the children of God, we are the biggest sect, for we are not standing in the position of brotherly love but exalting ourselves. The way of Philadelphia is the way we must take. The difficulty lies in the fact that Philadelphia includes all the brothers, yet some are not able to include as much.

Let me give you an illustration: Before the war with Japan I went to K'un-ming. There was a brother there of the _____ Church who asked me to talk with him. He was a very good brother. When he saw me he said, "Do you remember that I asked you a question in Shanghai? You still have not answered how we can cooperate." I said, "Brother, you have a _____ Church in which I have no part." He said, "Right, but you need not worry about that; what I mean is that we can cooperate nicely before the Lord." I said, "I have a church, and I am in it, Paul is in it, Peter is also in it, and so are John, Martin Luther, John Wesley, and Hudson Taylor. You too are in it. The church that I have is so great that all who are in Christ, whether great or small, are in it. You and I have a difference: I only build up one church; you wish to build up two churches. My work is only the church of Christ, not the _____ Church. If your aim is to build up the church of Christ and not the _____ Church, then I can absolutely cooperate with you." Brothers and sisters, do you see the difference here? That brother's love was not great enough. He stresses the church of Christ within the _____ Church. He is building up two churches. After I spoke he confessed that that was the first time he saw what it was all about. He held my hand and said that he hoped this question would not be raised again.

Brotherly love means that we must love all the brothers. If one has some weakness, that is another matter. I say that all the children of God must be baptized by immersion, but I cannot say that because one does not do it this way, he is not a brother. He is regenerated if he is immersed in water, and he is also regenerated if he is not immersed in water. We may regard his regeneration as the mistake of all mistakes, but my Father has begotten him. (The Lord forgive me for speaking in this way.) Indeed, when there is opportunity, we must read the Bible with him to let him know that the eunuch and Philip went down into the water and also that the Lord Jesus came out from the water (Acts 8:36-38; Matt. 3:16). Baptism in the Bible is man going down and man coming up, not just two fingers going down and coming up. But we cannot say that he is not a brother because he has not yet done this. The basis of being a brother is life, not baptism. Although we believe that baptism is right, we are not the Baptist Church. The basis of fellowship is the blood and the life of the Holy Spirit, not knowledge, not even the knowledge of the Bible. The only question is whether or not one has the life of God. If he has been regenerated, he is a brother. Loving one another is but to stand in this position. Whenever we bring in other things and add requirements, we are a sect. Consider the matter of the breaking of bread. Paul, a new believer, arrives in a certain place; someone has brought him there, and he really has a testimony. They know he is a brother, so he can break bread. There is absolutely no need for a second requirement. Does he believe that the great tribulation will last seven years? Is the rapture partial or whole? If we inquire of people in this way, we are basically wrong. If we only love the brothers who are the same as we are, we are sectarian, and this is contrary to the testimony of brotherly love. Thank God we are all brothers. Everyone redeemed by the precious blood is a brother. If something of ourselves comes out, it must be pride. Some say, "Only we are right; you brothers are all wrong." But the bread must include all the right as well as all the wrong brothers.

When you desire to follow the Lord in such a way, when you desire to love all the brothers, it does not mean that all the brothers will love you. You should realize this. Sardis came out from Thyatira. Although Sardis was following the will of the Lord, it is unavoidable that she would be hated by Rome. Likewise, just as Philadelphia came out from Sardis, the denominations will also be against you. Because they must maintain their organization, they will say that if you act in this way, you do not love your brothers. From their point of view, loving the brothers is equal to loving Sardis, as if loving the brothers and loving the denominations are not two different things. Those who have a motive to maintain the denominations will criticize your love as lacking because you are not building up their denominations. But you must be clear: Loving the brothers themselves and loving the denominations which these brothers love are two different things.

Moreover, we must realize that loving the whole church is simply based upon whether or not one is a brother; if one is a brother, we love him. This is loving the brothers. If we only love a part of all the brothers, then we are only loving the brothers who are within our circle. This kind of love for the brothers is not really love for the brothers, but love for division. If we do not abandon this love of sect, we cannot love the brothers. The love of sect is not only not right; it is positively wrong. Loving a sect is the greatest hindrance to loving the brothers. Unless a man rids himself of the love of sect, he cannot love the brothers. Yet a man who loves the brothers because he has no love of sect will be criticized by others as having no love. This is commonplace; do not think this is strange.

Let us bring up another point. Overcoming is spoken of in these epistles seven times. The Lord speaks to Ephesus: Repent. Overcoming depends on the discovery of the slackening of first love. The overcoming of Smyrna is nothing but the Lord's words: "Be faithful unto death, and I will give you the crown of life." In Pergamos the Lord is against the teaching of Balaam and the Nicolaitans; therefore, whoever rejects the teaching of Balaam and the Nicolaitans is an overcomer. In Thyatira there are still those who will not follow the teachings of Jezebel. The Lord says, "Hold fast until I come." This is overcoming. The Lord does not ask them to rise to be a Luther. In Sardis there are a few who are living. Although Sardis has nothing complete in herself, the Lord says that whoever is clothed in a white garment is the overcomer. To Philadelphia, although she has trials and hardships, the Lord remarkably says to hold fast that which she has; she has already overcome. As for Laodicea, it is not enough to just have the objective side; she must walk with the Lord subjectively. All of the overcoming refers to the differences among the children of God. The promises for overcoming are given to the churches; therefore, there are two kinds of people in the churches, the overcomers and the defeated ones. The separating point is that God has a plan, a standard. Whoever attains to the standard of God is an overcomer; whoever does not attain to the standard is not an overcomer. An overcomer merely does what he should do. Many have a wrong concept, thinking that overcoming means to be especially good. But remember, overcoming is the minimum degree; overcoming is not to rise above the level, but to come up to the level. If you are able to attain to this standard, you are an overcomer. To fail means that you are not able to reach the plan of God and you fall below the level.

I do not know how you feel, but today there is one thing that makes me very happy: God did not cause me to be born during the age of Thyatira, a period of almost 1,400 years. God also did not cause me to be born in the age of Sardis. We are born in this age, the age of Philadelphia, which has existed just over a hundred years. The Lord put us in the age of Philadelphia that we may be Philadelphia. Today there are many overcomers in Laodicea, but they are but overcomers in Laodicea. In the entire history of the church, there has not been an opportunity that is better than ours.

"He who overcomes, him I will make a pillar in the temple of My God, and he shall by no means go out anymore" (Rev. 3:12). We must pay attention to the word "anymore," which means to have gone out at least once. Among the brothers, eight out of ten have gone out before. The Lord's promise here is, I feel, very wonderful. If a pillar in the temple of God goes out again, the temple will collapse. The following three names are special: "The name of My God and the name of the city of My God, the New Jerusalem,...and My new name." What is the meaning of a name? There is great meaning in a name. The name of God represents the glory of God. Besides Philadelphia, no other church has received the glory of God. The name of the city of God is New Jerusalem. In other words, Philadelphia accomplishes the plan of God. *"My new name."* When the Lord Jesus ascended to heaven, He received a new name, a name that is above all names (Phil. 2:9-11). Here the Lord reveals that of all the churches, He especially fixes His eyes on Philadelphia. Today we thank God; we were born in an age in which we can be Philadelphia. Although we were born in an age in which the condition of the church is exceedingly confusing, thank God, we can be those of Philadelphia.

Finally, please remember that the Lord speaks the same words seven times to the seven churches: "He who has an ear, let him hear what the Spirit says to the churches" (Rev. 3:22). We have to pay attention to this word. The Lord's eyes are not only upon these seven churches; His eyes are also upon all the churches in the whole world, past and present, here and abroad. What the Lord says, He says to all the churches. The slackening condition found in the time of Ephesus is quite likely to occur in today's Philadelphia. Although the time of Smyrna has passed away, it is quite possible that it may occur again today. It is often possible for the condition of every church to occur in one church. The church is not that simple. Those special conditions are but the main conditions within a certain period of time. It is possible that all the conditions may occur in the seven churches at the same time.

The Lord says, "He who has an ear, let him hear what the Spirit says to the churches." Two people were walking on the street, and one said, "Just a moment, I hear the sound of crickets." His friend replied, "You are crazy; the cars in the street are making so much noise, we can hardly hear ourselves talking! How can you still hear the sound of crickets?" But he ran to the wall at the side of the street and told his friend to stand and listen. Sure enough, there was a cricket. His friend asked him how he could have possibly heard it. He replied, "Bankers can only hear the sound of money, and musicians can only hear the sound of music. I am an entomologist; my ear can hear the sound of insects." The Lord tells us that he who has an ear and can hear the Lord's word, let him hear. There are many who do not have ears and cannot hear the Lord's word. If we have an ear, we must hear. Pray that God will grant us to walk in a straight way. In any situation, no matter what happens, we must choose the way of Philadelphia.